# Testing and **Standards**

## A Brief Encyclopedia

**Sandra Wilde**

HEINEMANN
Portsmouth, NH

**Heinemann**

361 Hanover Street
Portsmouth, NH 03801–3912
www.heinemann.com

*Offices and agents throughout the world*

The author and publisher wish to thank those who have generously given permission to reprint borrowed material:

"SAT Prep" cartoon by Barbara Smaller is reprinted from the New Yorker Collection by permission of The Cartoon Bank, a division of *The New Yorker Magazine*. Copyright © 1998 by Barbara Smaller. All rights reserved.

"Test Preparation Activity" chart is adapted from "Raising Standardized Achievement Test Scores and the Origins of Test Score Pollution" by Thomas Haladyna, Susan Nolen, and Nancy Haas in *Educational Researcher*, 20. Adapted by permission of the American Educational Research Association.

"Concerning High Stakes Testing in PreK–12 Education" is reprinted by permission from the American Educational Research Association website,

**Library of Congress Cataloging-in-Publication Data**
Wilde, Sandra.
Testing and standards : a brief encyclopedia / Sandra Wilde.
     p. cm.
     Includes bibliographical references.
     ISBN 0-325-00360-2 (alk. paper)
     1. Educational tests and measurements—United States—Encyclopedias.
2. Education—Standards—United States—Encyclopedias. I. Title.

LB3051 .W4966 2002
371.26'4—dc21                   2002004352

Editor: Lois Bridges
Production service: Colophon
Production coordination: Vicki Kasabian
Cover design: Catherine Hawkes, Cat & Mouse
Typesetter: LeGwin Associates
Manufacturing: Steve Bernier

Printed in the United States of America on acid-free paper
T & C Digital

# Contents

# Acknowledgments

As always, great thanks go to Lois Bridges for her support, smarts, patience, and persistence. Susan Harmon and Susan Ohanian gave detailed and valued feedback on the manuscript. Thanks to the Urban Gals—Christine Chaillé, Emily de la Cruz, Sara Davis, Susan Halverson, and Micki Caskey—for professional support and laughs. I'm grateful to the staff at Redwood Terrace where my mother Anita Axelson lived for a year, especially Nancy Kress and Lisa Kukla. They did so much to take good care of her and ease my worries. Bill Kruger has provided important support and guidance.

I appreciate all the work of everyone at Heinemann and Colophon for all they've done to produce and market this book, especially Vicki Kasabian for being in charge and working with the cover design, and Denise Botelho for handling all the details of editing and production. I'm especially grateful that they were able to get the book into production so quickly. Heinemann is such a wonderful publisher!

# Introduction

Recently I spoke to a group of parents about testing and standards. After we examined some basic concepts about how standards are developed and what test scores mean, one of them said, "Why hasn't anyone ever told us this before?" Just like these parents, many teachers deal with the presence and consequences of testing and standards without knowing enough about them, particularly their technical aspects. Educators are expected to carry out policies that they haven't helped to develop and may not have the knowledge to fully assess. If these policies were benign, this might not be of such concern. However, standards and testing in these early years of the twenty-first century are increasingly taking on roles that violate good educational principles. Teachers need to be able to approach practices that don't seem to be in the best interest of their students with intelligent, informed critiques. This book was written to that end.

Some historical and cultural background: In recent years, both the educational community and the popular media have been filled with talk of state and national standards for education and the tests that are being instituted to ensure that students meet high standards.

Education, a public enterprise in the United States and elsewhere, has always been political, in the sense that it involves the spending of taxpayer funds to provide benefits to a country's residents. Those who serve us in government have, of course, a legitimate interest in ensuring that our money is being well-spent in educating the next generation of our communities. Increasingly, however, education is becoming not just political but politicized, as many politicians (as well as media commentators and others who echo them) have been demanding a greater role in the details of what public education should look like, looking to micromanage rather than relying on the professionals in the field. A cynic might say that this is due, at least in part, not to authentic knowledge about educational issues but to awareness of their potential as vote-getters.

The recent changes in educational policy often referred to as the "standards movement," under the broader rubric of "school reform," began during the Reagan administration with the publication of *A Nation at Risk* (National Commission on Excellent in Education 1983), a federal report lamenting the state of American education and linking it to dire economic predictions. Its tone is captured by a much-quoted line from its first page: "If an unfriendly foreign power had attempted to impose on America the mediocre educational performance that exists today, we might well have viewed it as an act of war" (5).

The present standards and testing landscape is a complex one. A key set of documents reflecting this are the annual reports, *Quality Counts,* which appear in the periodical *Education Week,* created in collaboration with the Pew Charitable Trusts (available online at http://www.edweek.org/sreports and published annually in January). This report assesses, among other indicators, the extent to which states have established academic standards and set up testing programs. The report gives each state a letter grade to rate its commitment to this agenda. The grade for standards and accountability is based on the extent and specificity of standards, what types of assessment measures are used, and the extent to which the standards carry high stakes (in this case, a high school exit exam).

The educational standards movement and the testing apparatus that goes with it constitute an increasingly massive and intricate system that involves many players, quite a few of them outside the classroom: local, state, and national politicians; the U.S. Department of Education and state departments of education; local school districts; textbook publishers; test publishers and developers (often the same companies who publish the textbooks); print, broadcast, and Internet media; and foundations and think tanks, to name only the most prominent players.

Where do classroom teachers and their students fit into this picture? For the most part, they're the objects of it, not the shapers of it. When state standards are put in place, decisions about what goes on in the classroom tend to be less often delegated to teachers than they had been before. If standards were merely a reflection of a universal consensus about what our students should be learning this would be less problematic, but teachers are often unhappy with the ways that standards and the testing that accompany them can narrow curriculum, emphasize knowledge that doesn't reflect current thinking in the field, and encourage teaching to the test. When testing is high-stakes for students, with a certain test score that is required for passing to the next grade or to graduate, standards affect not only how students spend their days in school but how long they spend there and how much their time there counts (in the sense that a student could work diligently and receive good grades all year but still not pass to the next grade).

My goal in writing this book is to help teachers, and by extension their students, to be less victimized by (indeed, to regain jurisdiction of their classrooms from) forces outside their control that are currently embodied in this standards and testing juggernaut. I have two goals.

First, it's crucial that we understand the concepts and vocabulary of testing and measurement to ensure that tests are being used appropriately. For instance, what does it mean to say that a test shows a student is reading at a fifth-grade level? What's the difference between a norm-referenced and a criterion-referenced test? This information is of course widely available, but what I've attempted to do here is to make it as accessible and user-friendly as possible.

Second, it's important for teachers to understand aspects of the wider context of standards and testing. Where do tests come from? What can they do and not do? What consequences do they have?

I've written this book in the form of a mini-encyclopedia, with brief essays on about thirty-five topics. You can dip into the book to inform yourself on a specific term or idea, or it can be read straight through as a quick primer on some of the concepts and issues involved in today's climate of standards and testing. Many of the examples come from the field of literacy, which I know best, and from Oregon, where I live, but the underlying principles and issues cut across subject areas and have surfaced across the country. Since my goals are modest ones, I've also provided an annotated bibliography of other writing on the topic, as well as some useful Internet links. (See **Essential Readings** and **Internet Resources**.)

Since my perspective is, you'll discover, a critical one, I wish to make it clear that yes, I think it's important that we have standards and expectations for the work of teachers and for student learning. And yes, it's crucially important to foster the learning of all students, and to work to decrease differences in achievement between rich and poor. However, we need to have lively debates about how this should take place and who should make decisions about it. In fact, I believe that many current testing and standards practices undermine rather than support these larger goals. This book is intended to be a contribution to that debate.

Alternatively, some readers may think I'm not being critical enough about testing. However, although I have serious, deep concerns about the underlying premises of today's testing apparatus, I think it's important also to understand when tests are and aren't legitimate when viewed on their own terms. Even if our ideal would be to eliminate these tests, we also need tools for challenging their abuse and misuse.

**What it means:** Taxpayers have a right to know that their education dollars are being well-spent.

**Example:** Schools should be willing and able to provide information about their programs and student learning to parents and other citizens.

### What you need to know about it

Who owns the public schools in a democracy? To whom are schools responsible? There's a current trend I find disturbing, a market analogy in which parents are seen as the "customers" of their children's education who, if they aren't happy with the "product," should be able for all practical purposes to pull their tax dollars out of the system (through voucher plans) and "shop" elsewhere. My lavish use of quotation marks here reflects how inappropriate I feel this metaphor is. For instance, it ignores the extent to which schools are educating children as members of the society as a whole, not just for the benefit of themselves and their parents. It also, when it becomes part of public rhetoric, reinforces the detachment of those who, having no children in school, feel little commitment to paying for education through their taxes (as we see in failed school bond measures).

Business—especially in its role as employer—is also viewed as a consumer of educational outcomes, in this case with students (i.e., potential employees) as the product. The standards and testing movement then becomes a quality control system, a *Consumer Reports* for parents wanting to know how the schools are doing (which is why realtors are a major audience for test scores) and for businesses wanting to ensure that their labor force meets specifications.

Although I believe that this consumer approach to education distorts some of the public dialogue about standards and testing, both parents and society at large do have the right to information about how our schools are doing. This isn't just a taxpayer issue.

Citizens have the right to know if the next generation is being well-prepared to function as full members of society. Parents also have the right to information about their own children's learning.

However, particularly at the state level, huge testing apparatuses are being put in place that attempt to do far too much: to serve as gatekeepers for individual students and also to tell the public how individual schools are doing and administrators how individual teachers are doing. Here are suggestions as to how we could accomplish reasonable aspects of accountability without some of the present problems of large-scale blitzes of testing that try to do everything at once:

1. Large-scale national assessments like the National Assessment of Educational Progress, which has been in place since 1969, can give us a sense of how our schools are doing overall, nationally and state-by-state as well as across time. Since these tests sample rather than assess all students, they're relatively efficient. Since they don't identify individual schools or even districts, they don't foster cheating.

2. At the state level, as an accountability snapshot, perhaps a single, relatively brief standardized test, could be used to keep tabs on schools and districts in a general way, and in particular to monitor for low-achieving schools. I'm a little hesitant to even recommend this given what we know about the limitations of standardized tests and how they've been abused, but here's how I think this could be done usefully.

First, pick a well-established test with the highest standards of validity and reliability. Second, make it clear that the results won't be used for any rewarding or punishing of schools or teachers. Third, administer it early in the school year to discourage teaching to the test. Fourth, don't report scores of individual students. Fifth, take demographics into account. Students in poorer communities, for a variety of reasons, have lower average test scores; equitable assessment of their progress needs to recognize their different starting point. Sixth, use the test to maintain records over time of schools' scores in order to look at change from year to year. Seventh, use the test as an indicator only, to suggest taking a closer look at schools that aren't doing as well as others in similar circumstances, or, more happily, to learn more about schools whose students are scoring better than one would expect. Eighth, provide full public disclosure of the costs of the tests in both money and classroom time. Without these safeguards, testing for accountability purposes can have multiple negative consequences and is subject to abuse, as described throughout this book.

3. As Grant Wiggins (1993) has suggested, schools and communities could explore a variety of ways to communicate not only how well local schools are doing, but what they uniquely offer students and their families. For instance, schools could assess themselves on their progress toward goals they've defined, with the state or community serving as an auditor of that assessment. At the very least, if test scores are used, reporting should focus on how they've changed or remained the same for that school over time, as an indicator of how well the staff has worked with what it's got, since just comparing test scores across schools privileges richer neighborhoods. But test scores alone are a narrow source of information compared to school portfolios, websites, newsletters, community nights, and so on.

4. Individual students are best assessed by the classroom teacher over time using a variety of measures. Books about and tools for student assessment are in plentiful supply. Professional organizations like the International Reading Association (IRA), the National Council of Teachers of English (NCTE), the National Council of Teachers of Mathematics (NCTM), and so on are excellent, reliable sources. (See **Group Versus Individual Assessment; Professional Organizations**.)

## authenticity in assessment

**What it means:** Evaluation that measures, as much as possible, what it claims to measure.

**Example:** Discussing a book with a student in order to assess whether she can understand what she's read.

### What you need to know about it

Let's think about students, say fifth-graders, learning to write. At this age, teachers hope that kids will be able to express their ideas comfortably, in a relatively organized way, with some sense of style and audience. We'd like them to be able to write in various genres: personal narrative, letters to the editor, simple research reports, simple fiction. We'd also like them to have reasonable proficiency in using the conventions of written language, which include writing that sounds like writing rather than just "writing the way they talk," as well as the smaller pieces of language like spelling and punctuation. We also, of course, realize that fifth-graders start the year at different stages of development as writers, depending on their interests and abilities as individuals as well as their previous experiences with writing, and that our expectations need to take this into account. Agreed?

However, how are we going to measure the extent to which students have met these goals? Imagine a continuum. Some standardized tests of writing (still common despite newer formats that ask students to write to prompts) use items such as the following:[1]

> Which underlined part of the sentence contains a mistake in spelling, word choice, or grammar?
>
> Everytime my mother asks my brother and me to run an errand, she talks in her nicest voice.

---

1. Because permission to reproduce test items in rarely granted, unless otherwise noted I've made up my examples of test items, but in ways that reflect actual practice.

4

a. Everytime
b. me
c. errand
d. talks
e. None of the above

Despite any claims that publishers of this kind of test might make about how well it correlates with assessments of students' actual writing, it doesn't feel authentic in the sense that it doesn't ask students to actually write. We realize that a student could be a good writer yet do poorly on this test, and vice versa.

Now imagine a teacher who has a good sense of what effective writing looks like as she reads a piece that a student wrote for some real purpose: a letter to his member of Congress about an issue he feels strongly about; a report based on his research on whales; a memoir of a favorite aunt. Imagine too that the teacher knows the student pretty well and has been involved in helping him develop as a writer over the past several months. This is about as authentic as it gets: We're assessing how well the student writes for a real purpose by looking directly at an example—and usually at multiple examples over time—of how well the student writes for a real purpose.

There's a wide range of possibilities between these two extremes of authenticity, and I'd like to suggest that you be very wary when you see a large-scale assessment (e.g., of all fifth-graders in the state) claim to be authentic, merely because it's in a format other than multiple-choice. The very features that make assessment more authentic make it less able to be carried out on a large scale. When students are asked to write in response to a topic, as they are now in many state writing assessments, it's easier to compare them to one another than if the topics were their own, but authenticity is decreased. Even though we want students to be able to write competently in response to assigned topics, part of what writers need to be able to do is to decide on and develop topics of their own.

Similarly, when teachers look at a wide range of student writing over the course of an academic year, work that varies not only in quality but in what is being attempted, their assessments have a greater authenticity than when a single piece of the student's writing is scored by a stranger.

In short, large-scale authentic assessment is at least to some extent an oxymoron. Or, put more precisely, state- or districtwide assessment based on a single day's efforts can never be more than minimally authentic.

This doesn't mean that small increases in authenticity don't matter. For instance, The National Assessment of Educational Progress (see page 47) assesses student spelling by determining the percentage of misspelled words in a composition written to a prompt (e.g., Donahue et al. 1999). Limited as this may be, it's certainly far more closely connected to the goal of having students spell well in their writing than is the typical standardized test item:

> Pick the correct spelling:
> a. accomodate  b. acommodate  c. accommodate
> d. acomodate

It also seems fairer and more precise, though of course more time-consuming and expensive, than asking a scorer to give a global score for conventions.

When students are asked to write on a state test, therefore, or to use math to figure out the solution to a problem, rather than merely bubbling in an answer sheet, these are somewhat more authentic tasks than the traditional alternatives, but still fall far short of what can be learned over time, across a variety of tasks, by a teacher who knows the student. This is particularly important when tests are used to make high-stakes decisions about individuals. (See **High Stakes; Group Versus Individual Assessment.**)

## carrot and stick
## (standards, testing, and motivation)

**What it means:** How do we get kids to want to learn?

**Example:** Carrot: Pass this test and get a good grade (or a sticker); Stick: Fail this test and get a bad report card (or repeat fourth grade).

### What you need to know about it

In an ideal world, all learning would be self-motivated. We'd learn because we're interested in a topic, because it helps us achieve some goal, or for the sheer joy of it. (In fact, a case can be made that we learn much of the time because we can't help it; Smith 1998.)

Why, then, do we spend so much time talking about motivation in schools? Obviously, it is because we don't live in an ideal world, and students aren't always interested in learning what we're trying to teach. This is, of course, an issue broad enough to fill a book of its own (and see Kohn [1993] for an illuminating book-length discussion on the topic of motivation generally and rewards in particular), but I'd like to make a few small points about how motivation can be mishandled in a standards-based curriculum.

The rhetoric of school reform is often about establishing high standards and having high expectations for students. So far so good. But in practice this often involves either requiring students to pass tests in order to progress through the grades or graduate, or sanctioning schools when not enough of their students pass the tests.

Thus a goal of learning because it's worth doing becomes a goal of learning because we expect it of you (or your students). And then this goal of learning because it's expected becomes a goal of passing a test in order to graduate (the carrot) or in order to avoid being retained in your grade (the stick). Similar carrots and sticks apply to teachers and schools. Not only does the motivation change from internal to external, but the focus changes from wanting to learn to wanting—indeed, needing—to get high test scores. Thus are cynicism and cheating born. (See **Ethics**.) And the pressure created by adding a new, more intense level of sanctions, coming from beyond the classroom, pulls everyone involved even further away from focusing on learning for its own sake.

## criterion- and norm-referenced tests

**What it means:** Criterion-referencing compares one to a standard; norm-referencing compares one to others.

**Example:** Criterion-referenced: How fast you run a mile. Norm-referenced: Did you come in first or tenth in a field of twenty?

### What you need to know about it

The distinction between criterion- and norm-referenced assessments is, for teachers, one of the most important concepts to understand in the field of testing and measurement. Let's look at examples of each and then explore some relevant issues.

Scores on the SAT test are an example of norm-referenced assessment. Here's how it works.[2] Scores on the SAT range from 200 to 800. A score of 500 means, roughly, that you did better than half the group that the test was normed on and worse than the other half. (The norming group is meant to represent a typical group of test-takers.) A score of 200 means that virtually everyone in that group did better than you. A score of 800 means that you did better than almost everyone else. Your score doesn't in itself say anything about how many answers you got right or wrong. (Thus a score of 800 isn't, as it's often referred to, a perfect score meaning that you got every answer right; it merely indicates, rather, that your score falls in the range achieved by the top 0.13 percent of test takers in the norming group; see **Standard Deviation**.)

2. This discussion has been somewhat simplified in order to give a broad outline of what a norm-referenced test entails.

A percentile score (see **Percentiles and Stanines**) gives similar information. A 500 SAT score is at the 50th percentile. You're at the 50th percentile for height if half the people (in a class, in the country, in your gender) are shorter than you and half are taller. Grading on a curve is also norm-referenced; your grade depends not on how many test items you got right, but on how many you got right compared to other students who took the test. This could be all the other students who took the test that day, or it could be all the other students who have taken the test in the past. A norm always implies, indeed requires, a norming group. (I once tutored a first-grader from a wealthy community who was an object of great concern since he had the lowest standardized reading test performance in his class. When I finally saw his scores, I discovered that he was right on the national mean. Compared to an elite group, he appeared to be in bad shape; compared to a more representative group, he was average.)

The number of pool lengths that you can swim without stopping is a clear-cut example of a criterion-referenced assessment. It is what it is, regardless of how any other swimmer did. The raw score of how many items you got right on a test is also a criterion-referenced measurement. A grading scheme that defines 90 to 100 percent correct as an A, 80 to 89 percent correct as a B, and so on is criterion-referenced.

These swimming and testing examples are, however, different in some important respects. Swimming is a direct measurement of swimming ability, since the performance itself is what we're interested in, but a test on, for instance, geometry, is only an indirect measure of the underlying knowledge that's presumably our real goal. For instance, the instructor might have inadvertently made the test too hard or too easy. Thus norm-referenced tests and practices like grading on a curve were designed to help compensate for the effects of inadequacies in the measurement tool.

The results of traditional standardized tests (such as the *Stanford Achievement Tests* and *Iowa Tests of Basic Skills*) are typically reported as normed references: percentiles, stanines, and grade-level equivalents are all ways of reporting where a test-taker stands in relation to others. However, many states currently, as part of their new standards-based approaches to education, have switched to a criterion-referenced test: This is what we want our students to know, and we're going to be measuring whether they know it. Student scores are determined not by how they did in comparison to others but by how many test items they got right (which may be stated as a raw score, a percentage, or a scaled score that makes comparisons across tests possible), or how their performance in an area like writing stood up against a rubric.

Although this may seem like a fairer form of assessment, it still has major pitfalls. The first is the difficulty of accurately measuring knowledge, particularly on a single, usually multiple-choice measure. Understanding the main idea of a book you've read isn't the same thing as reading a short passage and then picking out the correct main idea statement from four alternatives. (See **Reading Comprehension Assessment**.) One could argue about the extent to which they're closely related, but my point here is that they're not the same and that a test is at best an approximate measure of whether students have met the criterion we have in mind.

Second, since it's difficult even to measure whether a particular knowledge criterion has been reached, it's still more difficult to determine what a passing score should be. The public usually gets upset when what is perceived as too few or too many students pass a state test. If 95 percent pass, the bar must have been set too low; if 50 percent fail, it must have been set too high. The pressures to recalibrate are strong ones.

Ultimately, then, if passing scores end up being determined not by an objective judgment of how one knows whether a criterion has been reached but instead by what proportion of students should, for political reasons, be allowed to have passed, a criterion-referenced measure has metamorphosed into a norm-referenced one. (Susan Harmon [2001] suggests that we should refer to these as politically-referenced tests.) Similarly, as Gerald Bracey (2000a, 107) has pointed out, a norm-referenced test can be inappropriately used as a criterion-referenced one, as when the Chicago schools assigned a particular score on the *Iowa Test of Basic Skills* as a requirement for promotion to the next grade. Why is this inappropriate? Because rather than providing an accurate assessment that students haven't learned enough to proceed effectively to the next grade, the schools just assume this to be true of those who score lowest on a single test.

## curriculum alignment

**What it means:** Developing curriculum to fit a test.

**Example:** Spending considerable time practicing solving analogy questions (e.g., Pig is to oink as cow is to ??) because they appear on the state test.

### What you need to know about it

What relationship should there be between the tests that students take and the curriculum they're taught? In the case of classroom tests, this relationship is usually a simple one. The students are taught, then they're given a test based on the material they've covered. (This is, of course, only one, relatively narrow, example of the forms that classroom assessment might take.) With system-wide (district or state) tests, it's more complex.

Aligning a curriculum to match an upcoming test is considered unethical (Haladyna, Nolen, and Haas 1991; see **Ethics**). Perhaps even more centrally, curriculum theory is built around notions of what's valuable for students to learn, not the principle, "Find out what standardized test your students will be taking and develop your program around it." (Although this practice does of course take place.) But in today's standards-based climate, the picture is a little murkier.

In a typical standards-based system, a state department of education will define curriculum goals and then develop tests to match them. Particularly if the tests are high-stakes, teaching then tends to focus on what's being tested, with a rationale of "This is what our students are expected to know and what we're being held responsible for." However, there are problems with this approach.

Since testing is limited to what's measurable, as a result, curriculum and teaching may be as well. Even if standards are written relatively broadly, aspects of learning that are less easy to test will tend to be de-emphasized in the classroom because teachers will feel less accountable for them. In Oregon, six aspects of writing (ideas and content, organization, sentence fluency, voice, word choice, and conventions) were originally scored, and counted equally, in the state assessment, which asks students to write to a prompt. However, evaluation of voice and word choice were eventually dropped from the final score, because they were difficult to score consistently and in part because it seemed unfair to have them be a necessary condition of high school students' earning a mastery certificate (Hermens 2001; he is an official in the Oregon Department of Education). Also, the weight given to conventions in the final score was doubled. Voice and word choice remained part of the state's Common Curriculum Goals, but with no content standards or benchmarks attached to them (http://www.ode.state.or.us/tls/writing, as of April 2002). Presumably the state doesn't believe that these two characteristics are any less important in writing than they were originally, but the effect on classroom instruction is easy to imagine, particularly when there's administrative pressure to have standards be the central focus of instruction.

Also, if this model of establishing the standards, teaching to them, then testing them were to work reasonably well, it would require that the standards be of very high quality and reflect the best current thinking in their respective curriculum areas. Given political realities, however, this is unlikely. Standards developed by professional organizations in fields like mathematics, English language arts, and history have often been discounted by curriculum decision-makers for a variety of reasons (see **Professional Organizations**), while state governments, dependent on the good will of the public, have tended to write standards that are less innovative and more traditional, often focusing more on facts and skills and less on deeper knowledge and understanding.

## emotional aspects of testing

**What it means:** Students have feelings as a result of the tests they take.

**Example:** Tests, particularly when heavily emphasized, lead students to feel anxious, inadequate, or disillusioned more than a regular day in school does.

### What you need to know about it

Much of the public discussion of testing focuses on the tests, what they're supposed to measure, and the scores students receive on them. The experiences of test-takers, however, must also be considered.

Two *New York Times* reporters (Wilgorin and Steinberg 2000) interviewed 221 sixth-graders from twenty-one schools across the country and found that they were stressed and worried about school and about getting into college, and that standardized tests were high on their list of concerns. These students were well aware that such tests have higher stakes than ever: they were "far more worried than their predecessors that poor marks could land them in remedial classes, in summer school or even back to suffer sixth grade all over again next year."

Paris and coauthors (1991) surveyed one thousand students in grades 2 through 11 and raised similar concerns. The authors found that students grew more disillusioned and cynical about tests over time, became less interested in doing well, and often used strategies that were nonproductive (guessing) or inappropriate (cheating). Test anxiety was also a big issue. All of these patterns were more true of low-achieving students, suggesting not only that they're more damaged by tests but that results may be less valid for them.

Although teachers are less vulnerable than students, testing can have a negative impact on them as well. Mary Lee Smith (1991) conducted in-depth research at two elementary schools and found that testing had a variety of emotional impacts on teachers. They felt "shame, embarrassment, guilt, and anger" when test scores were published; alienated by the inadequacies of the tests coupled with the pressure to keep scores up; and anxious and guilty about the effects of testing on their students. (There were also effects on their teaching: there was less time available for instruction, the curriculum was narrowed, and the teachers' work was deskilled.)

These emotional consequences have to be considered when we talk about the pros and cons of testing. I agree with Paris and colleagues, who said, "A system of assessment could be designed that is both psychometrically and politically sound, but if it has a negative impact on students, it may not be educationally justifiable" (1991, 4). Anxieties and cynicism about testing aren't unavoidable concomitants of education but rather warning signs that we may be damaging the spirits of children and teachers.

## equity

**What it means:** Tests shouldn't have the potential to unfairly advantage or disadvantage members of one group in relation to another.

**Example:** Requiring a passing score on a single test for high school graduation is likely to disproportionately reduce the number of high school graduates from less privileged backgrounds.

### What you need to know about it

I remember hearing this story on National Public Radio several years ago. Ohio was among the first states to require a passing score on a test for high school graduation, regardless of whether you met all other graduation requirements and how good your grades were. A young African American woman spoke in tears of how, despite her years of hard work, she hadn't been allowed to "walk across the stage" at graduation. The shattering of her family's dream of participation in an important rite of passage and her sense of both betrayal and inadequacy were palpable.

Much has been written about differences in test scores between rich and poor and between different ethnic groups. (See Jencks and Phillips [1998], especially chapters 2 through 4, for a compilation of information and viewpoints.) In particular, there's been a good deal of discussion as to whether these differences are due to test bias or to actual disparities in learning and educational opportunity.[3] These are important questions; ensuring that tests have equivalent predictive value for all groups of examinees as well as ensuring that all students receive adequate schooling obviously continue to be major priorities. But what I'd like to focus on here are some effects of the testing juggernaut itself on economically disadvantaged students, many of them children of color.

First, since these students are in schools whose test scores tend to be below average, their teachers and principals are often under pressure to get the scores up, particularly today when testing has become so politicized. Note that I've said the pressure is to get the scores up, not (directly) to improve the quality of education. Supposedly, improved test scores are a sign of increased learning, but when the focus is on the scores, there's a temptation, frequently indulged, to engage in various forms of teaching to the test. Thus, as McNeil and Valenzuela (2000) have extensively researched and documented, throughout Texas, middle-class children, whose test scores are already higher, tend to receive normal kinds of instruction, but poorer children have been subjected to large amounts of test preparation drills that crowd out the regular curriculum. Such programs focus on low-level information and are severely out of

---

3. The reader should be aware that a third explanation, that there are inherent racial differences in intelligence (Hernstein and Murry 1994) has been thoroughly discredited. See, for instance, Fraser (1995) and Kincheloe, Steinberg, and Gresson (1996).

step with best educational practices. As Alfie Kohn (1999) has commented, the drive to raise test scores in poorer neighborhoods is often turning second-rate schools into third-rate ones. This is a far too common outcome when testing is high-stakes for school personnel; given a choice between improving education for their students and raising their test scores, if test scores are what counts, that's what many educators will go for.

A second concern is the equity issues that arise when testing is accompanied by high stakes for students, particularly in the form of graduation requirements. Through no fault of their own, students can do everything that's required of them in terms of attending, reading and learning  doing homework, and passing classroom tests, but still fail to pass on to the next grade or to graduate. Stories like the one in Ohio are becoming more and more common; this is echoed by an episode from a high school graduation ceremony described by McNeil and Valenzuela (2000):

> I attended [pseudonym] high school's graduation ceremony. In the middle of the ceremony after the class song was played, about eight students stood up to chant the words scrawled on a large banner they held in their hands: "14 YEARS OF SCHOOL. MADE IT THIS FAR. WHY CAN'T WE WALK?" After the students chanted these phrases several times, three cops and six ushers approached the crowd to take away their banners. The audience booed the cops, including all or most of the graduates sitting in their seats. The hundreds of boos, which included parents', brought the ceremony to a halt. Some students were escorted out of the audience by the police while others left on their own. I could clearly see how this state-level policy of linking the TAAS [Texas Assessment of Academic Skills] test to high school graduation was sensed by everyone as unjust. It was only too fitting to see how this policy was "policed" in a final show of force to the would-be high school grads. (Valenzuela's June 5, 1996 field notes)

The consequences are not just about disparities in the education of rich and poor and the concomitant waste of talent and opportunity. Such outcomes also damage the perceived (and of course actual) fairness and legitimacy of our school systems.

## essential readings

In the following annotated bibliography, I've focused mostly on book-length material that either provides valuable background information or makes a significant contribution to the current discussion on testing and standards. Further sources can be found in the reference list at the end of this book, including materials on more specific topics.

Berliner, David C., and Bruce J. Biddle. 1995. *The Manufactured Crisis: Myths, Fraud, and the Attack on America's Public Schools.* Reading, MA: Addison-Wesley.

A lengthy rebuttal to the conventional wisdom, beginning with *A Nation at Risk* (NCEE 1983), that American schools are failing. The authors' lengthy documentation draws on much of the same data that had been used to support more dire assessments. Their view that schools have been attacked for political purposes is controversial but should be read.

Bracey, Gerald W. 1997. *Setting the Record Straight: Responses to Misconceptions About Public Education in the United States.* Alexandria, VA: Association for Supervision and Curriculum Development.

In 1991, Gerald Bracey began his splendid series of "Bracey Reports" for the *Phi Delta Kappan*, in which he examined and shattered the prevailing mythology that American schools were in decline. He has now used the data that he drew on for those pieces to challenge eighteen of the most prevalent myths about American education, such as those declaring that test scores are plummeting and that teachers are incompetent.

Bracey, Gerald W. 2000. *Bail Me Out! Handling Difficult Data and Tough Questions About Public Schools.* Thousand Oaks, CA: Corwin.

Intended as a reference for educators coping with policy questions, Bracey's book is comprised of three parts: The first has to do with how to read and interpret statistical data, the second with principles and issues of testing, and the third with brief answers to specific questions, some of them test-related. This timely, readable book, more basic than Bracey's 1997 volume, is an outstanding primer on educational statistics and their relevance to current issues.

Falk, Beverly. 2000. *The Heart of the Matter: Using Standards and Assessments to Learn.* Portsmouth, NH: Heinemann.

This important book helps teachers think through good and bad aspects of standards, and explores ways to use them to support good practice in teaching and learning. It gives teachers the tools to regain ownership of the standards movement in the cause of student learning.

Harris, Joseph. 2000. *Get Ready! For Standardized Tests (Grade 4).* New York: McGraw-Hill. (With companion books, by various authors, for Grades 1 through 6.)

I've included this series of books, designed to help parents prepare their students for testing, because all the books include some valuable appendices: website addresses for each state department of education and its testing programs, as well as a list, by state, of whether tests are criterion-referenced, norm-referenced, or performance-based, as well as the years in which students are tested. I can't help but note, however, the irony that McGraw-Hill, a major test publisher, is now also profiting by developing these coaching books for kids and parents who are dealing with the test anxiety that McGraw-Hill helped create.

Hill, Clifford, and Fric Larsen. 2000. *Children and Reading Tests* (Advances in Discourse Processes, Vol. LXV). Stamford, CT: Ablex.

Although this book may seem daunting since it's the lengthy report of a research study, it's a fascinating exploration of children's responses to standardized test items. The authors conducted interviews with children who had responded to test items, examining how they understood what they'd read. Very often, their incorrect test responses revealed that they didn't have reading problems but merely understandings that differed from those of the test makers. For instance, one item described a family who "took a bus across town to the train station" while leaving on a vacation, and asked where their home was. One student who picked "in a little town" rather than "in a city" explained his response as follows: "If it was in the city, it would say 'take a bus across the city'" (58).

Hopkins, Kenneth D. (1998). *Educational and Psychological Measurement and Evaluation* (8th ed.). Boston: Allyn and Bacon.

For those interested in the technical aspects of matters such as standard scores, stanines, grade-level equivalent scores, and so on, a textbook such as this one provides information that's particularly useful if you want a deeper understanding of the meaning and interpretability of the scores themselves.

Kohn, Alfie. 1999. *The Schools Our Children Deserve: Moving Beyond Traditional Classrooms and "Tougher Standards."* Boston: Houghton Mifflin.

Kohn, Alfie. 2000. *The Case Against Standardized Testing: Raising the Scores, Ruining the Schools.* Portsmouth, NH: Heinemann.

Kohn, a writer well-known for his work on the drawbacks of competition and rewards in education, is an activist who has written and spoken widely on the dangers of inappropriate testing. *The Case Against Standardized Testing,* the shorter of these two books, is a quick read (sixty-six pages) that deals concisely, in a Q&A format, with all the important concerns that have been raised about standardized tests. It was adapted in large part from *The Schools Our Children Deserve* (1999), a lengthier discussion of educational issues that was designed to reach a wide audience.

Lemann, Nicholas. 1999. *The Big Test: The Secret History of the American Meritocracy*. New York: Farrar, Straus & Giroux.

This excellent, exhaustive recent history of the SAT shows how a test that was originally designed to help worthy students from more modest backgrounds has merely helped to perpetuate another kind of elite. Although the roots of the SAT are in the elite Ivy League, it now also affects the great majority of students who attend other kinds of colleges.

Ohanian, Susan. 1998. *Standards, Plain English, and the Ugly Duckling: Lessons About What Teachers Really Do*. New York/ Bloomington, IN: Phi Delta Kappan Educational Foundation.

Ohanian, Susan. 1999. *One Size Fits Few: The Folly of Educational Standards*. Portsmouth, NH: Heinemann.

Susan Ohanian is perhaps the most passionate as well as the funniest writer (much of it is black humor) on standards and testing today. Her years of experience as a teacher have made her bitingly critical of the "Standardistos" who think that measuring students more will help them learn better. These two brief books are written from the perspective of a teacher who knows that kids can't be crammed into pigeonholes.

Rothstein, Richard. 1998. *The Way We Were? The Myths and Realities of America's Student Achievement*. New York: The Century Foundation.

Rothstein, now an education columnist for the *New York Times*, shows that not only is student achievement not declining, but also that pundits have been clamoring for decades for a return to a previous golden age of educational achievement that in fact never existed. Rothstein also takes a close look at varied evidence about matters such as minority achievement, social promotion, and bilingual education to show that much current discussion misinterprets not just the data but the history of these issues.

Sacks, Peter. 1999. *Standardized Minds: The High Price of America's Testing Culture and What We Can Do to Change It.* Cambridge, MA: Perseus.

If you would like to read a single lengthier book about testing, this is the one that I'd strongly recommend. A seasoned journalist, Sacks takes a comprehensive look at the role of testing in American schools and society, examining its history, pervasiveness, and effects. His book, aimed at the general public rather than educators, deserves a wide audience.

Swope, Kathy, and Barbara Miner, eds. 2000. *Failing Our Kids: Why the Testing Craze Won't Fix Our Schools.* Milwaukee, WI: Rethinking Schools.

An outstanding compilation of articles collected from the previous few years' issues of the activist education magazine *Rethinking Schools.* The authors include many classroom teachers, as well as parents, students, activists, and researchers, who react, analyze, and suggest alternatives to testing. This is a particularly good book to read for those who are concerned with issues of equity, social justice, and political critique.

Taylor, Kathe, and Sherry Walton. 1998. *Children at the Center: A Workshop Approach to Standardized Test Preparation, K–8.* Portsmouth, NH: Heinemann.

The authors of this useful handbook take the sensible view that teachers have a responsibility to make sure that students are "testwise" so that the knowledge they have will show up clearly when they take a standardized test. This is a refreshing change from approaches whose focus is drill on the potential content of the tests. Taylor and Walton help teachers to develop workshops that help students know how to deal with tests by thinking actively about them as texts that have a specific format that can be understood and negotiated. Another book that takes a similar approach is *A Teacher's Guide to Standardized Reading Tests* (Calkins et al. 1998).

Wiggins, Grant. 1993. *Assessing Student Performance: Exploring the Purpose and Limits of Testing*. San Francisco: Jossey-Bass.

This is among the most thoughtful considerations available of how we can best assess student learning and performance, as well as developing useful measures of accountability. (Wiggins, in fact, points out that individual teachers are currently for the most part *immune from* accountability [263].) Wiggins has thought deeply about the impact that assessment measures have on learning, and has excellent proposals for educators and the public to consider.

And, finally, three children's books:

Cohen, Miriam. 1980. *First Grade Takes a Test*. New York: Greenwillow.

Finchler, Judy. 2000. *Testing Miss Malarkey*. New York: Walker.

Seuss, Dr., and Jack Prelutsky. 1998. *Hooray for Diffendoofer Day!* New York: Knopf.

Two of these books delightfully satirize testing in schools. The students at Seuss and Prelutsky's Diffendoofer School (1998), whose teachers "make up their own rules," and have a very unconventional curriculum, get very nervous when they discover a big high-stakes test is coming. Similarly, the students of Finchler's Miss Malarkey get quite discombobulated about the testing machinery that's heading their way. Both stories, however, end with the students' getting high test scores, therefore blunting the books' bite. Cohen's much more modest book, part of a series about a first-grade class, is quite charming in showing how young children interpret test items with their six-year-old minds, and ends with a recognition that there's lots of knowledge that doesn't show up on a standardized test.

**What it means:** Do schools, teachers, and students avoid dishonesty that would compromise the accuracy or meaningfulness of test results?

**Example:** Teaching how to bubble-in answer sheets: Okay. Giving extra time on a timed test: Not okay.

### What you need to know about it

Remember when it was just the students who cheated on tests?

As testing mania has increased, and in particular as teachers and administrators have been rewarded and punished on the basis of their students' test scores, cheating incidents have been in the news. From New York we hear that nine educators were fired after a teacher reported that test answers were being supplied to students (Hartocollis 2000). Testing officials discovered that in Houston, incorrect answers had often been suspiciously erased and replaced with correct ones. Also in Texas, the Austin school district and an administrator were charged with tampering (Hartocollis 1999).In Maryland, the principal of an already high-scoring school resigned after accusations of not only giving extra time for tests but providing answers. (*Newsweek*'s acerbic report on the episode [Thomas and Wingert 2000] quoted a fifth-grader: "I think [the principal] just wanted to get first place. . . . I think she should have let us try our hardest and see if we could get first place on our own.")

Everyone, of course, deplores cheating, especially by those entrusted with the education of the young. It's intrinsically wrong, it sets a horrible example, and it damages the legitimacy and accuracy of the tests. These episodes that made the news are all clear violations of testing ethics. But where should the line be drawn? What counts as reasonable test preparation and what crosses over into cheating?

See what you think. For each of the cases in the following chart, check off whether you think it's ethical behavior for a teacher or principal. Assume, for these purposes, that the scores from the tests involved will be used to assess the effectiveness of teachers and schools and that the test is a typical standardized test rather than one written to reflect your curriculum.

| | Ethical | Unsure | Not ethical |
|---|---|---|---|
| 1. Spend a month prior to the test, for a healthy part of the school day, reviewing the topics that are likely to be covered on the test. | | | |
| 2. Encourage students to get a good night's sleep and have a good breakfast before the test. | | | |
| 3. Read over the actual test that will be administered and teach the content of specific items. | | | |
| 4. Use the test to plan your curriculum for the year. | | | |
| 5. Make sure students know how to bubble-in answer sheets. | | | |
| 6. Give students a little extra time on a timed test so they won't feel frustrated that they haven't been able to finish. | | | |
| 7. Clean stray marks off machine-graded answer sheets and darken faint ones. | | | |
| 8. Coach a student who's about to erase a correct answer. | | | |
| 9. Excuse low-achieving students from tests. | | | |

Although the examples are my own, I follow the principles of Haladyna, Nolen, and Haas (1991) in stating that only items 2, 5, and 7 are considered ethical. Even the ethical activities can be problematic if they're applied to only some of the students being tested, since this can slant the results in ways that have nothing to do with what's being tested.

Here's a table that Haladyna and his co-authors provide:

## A Continuum of Test Preparation Activities

| Test Preparation Activity | Degree of Ethicality |
|---|---|
| Training in testwiseness skills | Ethical |
| Checking answer sheets to make sure that each has been properly completed | Ethical (if done for all students) |
| Increasing student motivation to perform on the test through appeals to parents, students, and teachers | Ethical |
| Developing a curriculum based on the content of the test | Unethical |
| Preparing objectives based on items on the test and teaching accordingly | Unethical |
| Presenting items similar to those on the test | Unethical |
| Using Scoring High [a commercial test-preparation program] or other score-boosting activities | Unethical |
| Dismissing low-achieving students on testing day to artificially boost test scores | Highly unethical |
| Presenting items verbatim from the test to be given | Highly unethical |

(from Haladyna et al. 1991; reprinted by permission)

Many educators may be surprised to see that the kinds of content review that are common during the part of the school year immediately before testing are considered inappropriate. Don't we want our students to do well on tests? Well, yes and no. Although we want them to do well, this is really shorthand for saying that we want them to learn and then we want an accurate assessment to show that they have indeed learned. Practices that attempt to boost student performance on tests (rather than focusing on learning an appropriate curriculum) lead to inaccurate and indeed dishonest test results. Proper test preparation is best limited to making sure that students have a fighting chance to show off the knowledge that they do have: that is, that they are well-rested, understand the appropriate role of guessing if they aren't sure of the answer, and so on. Ironically, the emotional impact of intense, unethical test preparation may be to make students so worried and upset that they do less well than they would have otherwise.

States will be well-advised to adopt clear-cut ethical policies for testing. See, for instance, those established by the Michigan Merit Award Board (2000), which lists thirty-four very explicit unethical practices, such as "the classroom review of [state]-test skills, strategies, and concepts to the exclusion of concentration on the total curriculum."

## gain scores and value added

**What it means:** Changes in an individual's or school's test scores from year to year.

**Example:** This year, School A's test scores averaged out to the 90th percentile and School B's to the 50th. But last year, however, they were at the 95th and 45th percentiles respectively, so School B has actually done better in the past year.

### What you need to know about it

Several years ago, a friend of mine who was a principal in a large school system told me how discouraged she was feeling. Once again, she'd been called on the carpet when the annual test scores were released. Her school, in a largely white working-class rural area on the edge of the city, typically scored below average. The scores themselves, not what she'd accomplished, were what mattered to my friend's boss, and the principals of schools in wealthier parts of town whose students scored higher were much more appreciated by the central office.

Don't we want and expect all students to achieve? Of course, but we have to realize that student learning is affected not only by school experiences but by everything else that's part of their lives. Imagine two children with equivalent native ability entering kindergarten. One has well-off parents with graduate degrees who succeeded in school themselves. They can afford a good preschool, books, and travel for their child. The other child's parents never finished high school and work in blue- or pink-collar jobs that leave them exhausted at the end of the day. Books are expensive luxuries and there's little time for library visits. English may be their second language.

If these two students were given standardized tests the first day of school, their scores would be different, even if the children were equal in ability, interest in learning, personal qualities like persistence and hard work, and how much their parents value education. The score differences would be a result of their disparate exposure to experiences that provide the kind of learning that's valued in schools and on tests. This is, of course, without taking into account other differences between rich and poor children that arise from variations in nutrition, stress, medical care, and so on.

Then imagine a good school in a poor neighborhood where teachers work hard and students grow and learn every year, yet test scores are still below average because the children were less advanced to start with. And imagine too a school in a rich neighborhood where the faculty have grown complacent because their kids will have high test scores no matter what. Also, remember that the differences in opportunities for academic learning outside of school persist and add up throughout the years of schooling, up through high school—when only some kids can afford SAT prep courses—and beyond. You can imagine the frustration of the good teachers in the poor neighborhood who have dedicated themselves to working in a challenging setting yet continue to be reproached for their students' low test scores.

Goals that are identical for all, like "every child reading at grade level by third grade" sound fair and democratic, yet end up privileging those who are already privileged and punishing those who are already behind, even if they and their teachers work hard. This is why, in Grant Wiggins' term (1993), we should look to schools for their "value added" performance; that is, how well they've done with the students they have.

Ideally (and taking into account all the limitations of standardized tests discussed elsewhere in this book) an equitable measure would be to look at each student's learning growth from one year to the next, and average that for all the students in a school. Since some schools, particularly in poorer neighborhoods, have high turnover rates, in some cases more than 100 percent, it would seem fairest to include in any cross-school comparison only students who'd been at a school all year. (Of course even such a measure wouldn't take into account students' out-of-school learning opportunities.)

However, I think the point is clear. At the very least, when student achievement is being assessed for the purpose of seeing how well our schools are doing, we need to pinpoint as much as possible what the schools, as opposed to everything else in children's lives, are doing to bring about learning. One way to do this is to look at gain scores, which is what this year's fourth-graders know compared to what they knew last year in third grade. Another is to report scores to the public in a way that ensures that schools are compared to others with similar demographic profiles.

This issue is a touchy and difficult one, because we risk making it look like it's okay for some kids to know less than others and perhaps to fall further behind every year. Yet in the day-to-day life of classrooms, we don't focus on how students compare to all the others in the city or the country: We're appropriately seeing them and taking them as they are and where they are, and spending the five or six hours a day we have with them helping them to develop from that point. That's the appropriate focus of schools, and what they can best be held accountable for.

## grade level

**What it means:** In the context of standardized testing, grade-level equivalents are another way of reporting norm-referenced scores; that is, how a student compares to other students in the same grade of school.

**Example:** A fourth-grade student who does well on a standardized math test may be assigned a grade equivalent score of 6.5. This means that she did better than the average fourth-grader; it does *not*, however, mean that she could or should be doing sixth-grade math.

### What you need to know about it

"Every child reading at grade level" has become a mantra, especially for politicians. Who could quarrel with it? But when we unpack the meaning of this phrase, we can see the problem with it, the result of two different meanings of "grade level" being conflated and confused.

What the politicians intend to mean is that all students should be able, for instance, by third grade to read books that educators would agree are those that are worthwhile for them to read at that age. We also know how socially important it is for kids to be able to read the books that their friends are reading. We've all seen students pretending to read *Goosebumps* books that are way too hard for them because it's important to be perceived as a *Goosebumps* reader.

Although this intended grade-level reading goal may not be realistic, since students and resources vary, it's certainly admirable. The problem comes with how it's defined operationally.

There are two possible ways to define a student as "reading at a third-grade level." The first is to determine that a book is at a third-grade reading level (if, in fact, that can be defined satisfactorily) and see if a student can read it. This is the principle behind Informal Reading Inventories (e.g., Burns 1998), designed primarily to place students in an appropriate level of basal reader (reading series textbook). A readability formula, based usually on word length and/or word frequency plus sentence length, can be applied to a passage to establish a grade level. These formulas are at best only approximate, although the Dale-Chall formula (as cited in Hopkins 1998) is designed to identify the grade at which students will be able to answer 50 percent of the comprehension questions on a passage correctly.

In a variation on this, in a policy that seems to wildly sacrifice reliability in an attempt to be more authentic, Oregon's state assessment expects students to read a grade-level passage aloud at prescribed levels of accuracy, fluency, and comprehension, but the texts were chosen by asking teachers throughout the state to recommend books that students at the benchmark years should be able to read. For third grade, these included the well-known children's books *Lon PoPo* (Philomel, 1989), *Mufaro's Beautiful Daughters* (Lothrop, Lee, and Shepard, 1987) and *Ramona Forever* (Morrow, 1984), for which I assessed reading grade levels of 2/3, 5, and 6, respectively (using the Fry readability formula, available widely on the Internet). Not only is the selection of the texts mostly inappropriate, the assessment is completely unreliable. (See **Reliability**.) A teacher could easily inflate the number of her students meeting the benchmark by having them all read from the easiest of the books, or cause many of them to fail by inadvertently choosing the hardest one.

However, in practice, the grade level at which students are reading for large-scale assessment purposes isn't usually established by having students read aloud, nor is there an equivalent to readability formulas in other subject areas. In practice, reading or doing math or science at grade level is usually defined as receiving a score on a standardized test whose grade-level equivalent matches the grade that you're in.

How is this determined? Grade equivalent scores for fifth grade range from 5.0 to 5.9, with the numeral after the decimal point corresponding to the month of the school year. If the test was administered to the norming group at the beginning of the school year, whatever score was obtained by the average test-taker would be defined as a 5.0 grade equivalent. The average grade-equivalent score for a fifth-grader taking the test in April (of a September to June school year) would be 5.7. This is *all* that a grade-equivalent score means. It has no direct relationship to what educators feel fifth-graders should know or be able to do, but is merely a statement of how this student compares to other fifth-graders.

We see now the fallacy of the goal of all students achieving at grade level if this is how grade level is defined operationally. It's the equivalent of saying that all students should reach the average height. Even if, unrealistically, all students could reach today's average height or reading ability, the measures would have to be renormed eventually and half of students would again fall below the average.

In addition to this very basic definitional problem with grade-level equivalents, there's a technical problem when students score appreciably above or below the mean. For elementary school in particular, standardized tests are designed for and normed on a relatively narrow age range. Grade-level equivalents for high and low scores are established by extrapolation, which is a statistical projection. For instance, if a fifth-grader receives a grade-level equivalent score of 8.0 on the fifth-grade test, it doesn't mean she reads as well as a typical eighth-grader, since eighth-graders weren't part of the norming group for the test, and at any rate the test was made up of fifth-grade rather than eighth-grade reading material. But the grade equivalent score of 8.0 could mislead parents into thinking their child should be placed in an eighth-grade classroom for reading, or at least read the same books that eighth-graders do.

Given how misleading grade-level equivalent scores can be, there's a good case to be made for avoiding their use entirely. They're used, of course, because they seem less technical than other ways of reporting scores on normed tests, particularly to parents, but this accessibility comes at the price of inaccuracy. At the very least, when politicians and school administrators set achievement at grade level as a goal, we should insist that they define precisely what they mean and how they're going to measure it.

## group versus individual assessment

**What it means:** Different methods and standards should be used for assessing individuals and for assessing groups.

**Example:** Assessing a city population's health can be done through statistics (drug sales, hospitalizations) and surveys, but assessing an individual's health requires a fair amount of time with that individual, particularly when treatment decisions are involved.

### What you need to know about it

In educational assessment, sometimes we want to know how individual students are doing, while at other times we want to know how a larger group, such as a school, state, or country, is doing. We have to be much more careful when we use test data to make decisions about individuals.

Take the SAT test as an example. (I'm refering here to the SAT-I, the verbal and math rather than subject-area test.) SAT scores are used in the real world for a variety of purposes, including (often inappropriately) as an indicator of how our schools are doing (see

SAT Tests) and as a measure of how selective a college is, but their intended purpose is to serve as a guideline for college admissions offices by predicting likely academic success in the first year of college. (The SAT was originally designed, in fact, to help provide access to elite colleges for talented students from modest backgrounds [Lemann 1999].) This is a reasonable use of a test score for making a decision about an individual, but since its predictive value is far from absolute (the correlation between SAT scores and freshman grades is about 0.42 according to an ETS study [Sachs 1999, 270], not 1.00), it's used most appropriately in conjunction with other information about a student, not as a strict cutoff.

We can all think of cases when a high SAT score doesn't mean that a student will do well in college (a bright student who doesn't like to work hard) or vice versa (a student who doesn't "test well" but shines on essay exams and projects). Fairness therefore suggests that admissions offices shouldn't put more reliance on this single score than it deserves. When looking at the SAT scores of a whole group, however, like the average for an entering freshman class, these cautions are far less important, partly because testing error will average out, but also because the number won't be used to make a thumbs-up or thumbs-down decision about any individual.

Standardized tests have been used for years to provide information about schools, districts, states, and countries, and testing at the district and state level has usually involved reporting of scores to parents, often without adequate explanation of their meanings. However, what's new, and troubling, is the misuse of tests that may be adequate for comparing groups of students in using them to make high-stakes decisions about individuals.

A single test is unlikely to provide adequate information for making an important decision about a student, even when measurement error is compensated for by allowing the student to retake the test. The National Commission on Testing and Public Policy (1990) provided a powerful illustration of this. They point out that a typical test designed to predict performance does so with about a 0.35

correlation. They then show the effects of this on a hypothetical group of 1,000 people, 80 percent of whom would be able to perform successfully on the job or in school. If a cutoff score on the test (pegged to that 80 percent figure) served as a gatekeeper, 800 would pass the test, of whom 672 would actually do well. Of the 200 who failed the test, however, about 132 (or two-thirds of them) would be capable of performing adequately. For a test with typically low predictive value, therefore (and if most test-takers meet the criterion the test is measuring for), most test-takers who "fail" and are therefore barred from the next grade or from a job have actually received false negative scores and have been unfairly treated.

Multiple assessment tools are typically used for placing students in programs like gifted or special education at least in part because of these limitations of test scores. Of course, in the case of many of today's tests that are given to all students, there isn't even an attempt to establish predictive value. And even if failing a fourth-grade test predicts that you're unlikely to do well in fifth grade, does repeating fourth grade mean you're more likely to succeed in the long run? This isn't like college admissions where a student whose test scores aren't high enough for Harvard can get a perfectly good education at the University of Arizona. If you're kept out of fifth grade, repeating fourth grade is your only choice.

Even more problematic, does refusing a student a high school diploma for failing a test serve some useful purpose by keeping the student out of a job that requires a high school eduation? Is there any relationship between the test and likely performance on such a job?

The public therefore must be extremely vigilant in monitoring the impact of test scores on individual students. Although it may seem like there's been a minor change from reporting both school and individual scores on a test to actually using those scores to make decisions about students, it reflects a major policy shift since individual scores are so much less reliable than scores aggregated for a whole group. And students can't opt out unless they can afford private school. A compulsory education system, paid for by tax dollars, cannot be allowed to make such important decisions about people so casually and with so little evidence.

## high stakes

**What it means:**  A test score has some real effect on your life.

**Example:**  If you fail the test, you don't go on to fifth grade.

### What you need to know about it

A high-stakes test is simply defined as one whose outcome serves as a decision point for some concrete outcome in life—one does or doesn't get a barber's license, get arrested for drunk driving, get credit for a course, and so on. In some cases there's a cutoff score—excellent performance on the road test can't compensate for failing the vision exam at Motor Vehicles—while at other times the test is part of a continuum (your school is in the top 25 percent) or is considered along with other factors (good grades will help compensate for a lower SAT score).

Although high-stakes tests have been common for some time in higher education and for entering professions like the law, their use in K–12 public education is relatively new. They apply to students when a low test score results in not passing or graduating (though summer school or a retaking of the test are often available as options). High stakes can also apply to teachers and administrators; although they've been used as part of teacher evaluation and published in the newspaper in the past, what's new here is the more formal high stakes, still relatively rare, of linking educators' salaries or even their continued employment to test scores.

What's of concern isn't the idea of high expectations for students and teachers, but the exaggerated emphasis put on a single measure. Consider some possible unintended consequences: alienation on the part of students who feel their year's work counts for little; large numbers of students retained in grade; teaching to the test and other ethical violations; lack of perceived legitimacy and fairness.

There aren't many other areas of life where a single test can have so much impact. Generally in school, teacher-made tests usually make up only part of a grade. Job performance is assessed on multiple measures. Some colleges don't even require the SAT anymore, and those that do look at grades and other factors as well. For high-stakes tests that impact a wide range of the public, like the written driver's exam (which one usually only has to take once in a lifetime or when moving to another state), the bar is set relatively low, and those who speak other languages or aren't literate are accommodated. The few examples in everyday life of true high-stakes tests typically accompany professions such as law (the bar exam) and beauty salon work, where the public welfare has to be protected. But these are connected with freely-chosen lines of work, not compulsory public education.

For the teachers of our students also, it's not fair to put so much emphasis on a single measure, since only some (unknown) proportion of students' test scores is attributable to the quality of teaching they've received.

Why such an emphasis on high-stakes testing for children when it isn't common in the rest of our culture? It seems at times to reflect a get-tough stance: "Let's not let these lazy students and their grade-inflating teachers get away with it." Ironically, when legislators and other elected officials in Florida were invited to take their state's high-school graduation test and have their scores published in the newspaper, they all declined (Hegarty 2000).

A useful resource, particularly for activists who want to hold testing agencies accountable for appropriate use of high-stakes tests, is the book *High Stakes: Testing for Tracking, Promotion, and Graduation* (Heubert and Hauser 1999). This important report was prepared by the Committee on Appropriate Test Use and the Board on Testing and Assessment of the National Research Council, which is part of the National Academy of Sciences. This prestigious group was commissioned by Congress to establish appropriate standards for the use of high-stakes testing in the United States. Its final chapter of findings and recommendations represent an unassailable gold standard for test policies and practices. In general, they emphasize throughout that high-stakes decisions need to be made very carefully and with the highest possible attention to accuracy and equity. (See also the position of the American Educational Research Association on High-Stakes Testing, which appears as the Appendix of this book.)

## how much do tests cost?

**What it means:** Tests cost money directly (to develop or purchase and score) and indirectly (in student and teacher time).

**Example:** Although test booklets and scoring cost just a few dollars each, one Texas school spends almost $20,000, most of its institutional budget, for test preparation materials (McNeil 2000, 236).

### What you need to know about it

Testing is clearly a big business. It makes money for test developers and administrators (including private companies like publishers and nonprofits like the Educational Testing Service). Those who publish test-taking guides and offer workshops that promise to boost your scores also profit. Some of these costs are paid directly by the test-takers, particularly for entrance or gatekeeping exams like the SAT. But since public agencies like state departments of education and school districts devote large amounts of time and resources to testing, taxpayers are responsible for a great deal of the cost.

As more and more states institute their own tests, costs rise every year. Haney, Madaus, and Lyons, writing in 1993, did a detailed cost analysis that helped to illuminate what the finances of testing look like in terms of costs per hour of testing. Considering typical prices for major commercially-published test batteries plus scoring services, they arrived at a range of 75 cents to a dollar per hour of testing. (The figure would presumably be higher for a state's own tests, since development costs would tend to be more expensive than buying ready-made tests.) Haney and his colleagues also, however, tabulated an indirect cost per hour of test time, based on the value of the teacher and student time spent in test preparation to the exclusion of more meaningful learning. This is a bold approach, since it attempts not only to tabulate actual costs but to assign a monetary value to how much an hour of school time is worth to a student. But it's a useful avenue for estimating what would otherwise be unmeasurable. Their estimate of indirect cost of state testing ranged from a low of $3.49 per student per hour of testing to $65.39. (The details of how they arrived at their figures are too complex to summarize here, but the chapter is well worth seeking out and reading.)

The cost of state testing programs is often rationalized as a relatively inexpensive tool for finding out how students are learning. But as Haney and his coauthors suggest, aside from issues of whether such tests are indeed accurate touchstones, we must also take into account the costs in student learning if test preparation, particularly the extensive teaching to the test that has become so common, is allowed to drive out other, probably better use of instructional time.

Linda McNeil (2000) has documented what this looked like in one school district. She begins her book, *Contradictions of School Reform*, primarily as a portrait of the powerful successes created in several magnet schools that combined excellence with equity in a large school district in Texas. Despite numerous obstacles, both in the conditions of student lives and in the educational system, dedicated teachers and students in the right kind of supportive environment were able to create rigorous, meaningful educational experiences.

However, the second half of her book describes how an extensive, top-down statewide standards and testing movement, originated by (among others) Ross Perot and continued by former Governor George W. Bush, had a devastating impact through imposition of control and narrow expectations. Good teachers were forced to choose between a curriculum they believed was meaningful and a curriculum that would help their students pass the state tests. (Administrators often enforced the latter, leading some teachers to create dual lesson plans.) The curriculum "proficiencies" listed by the state were created not out of a sense of best practice in the field but to fit the subject area into boundaries testable in a multiple-choice format (McNeil 2000, 199). Schools were especially likely to channel students of color into courses that were primarily test preparation, to retain students as a way of raising a grade's test scores, and even to encourage or avoid discouraging drop-outs. McNeil's heartbreaking book reminds us of how seriously we must take all the costs of any testing program; these are serious public policy matters that should only be undertaken with informed public input and consent.

## Internet resources

Out of the extensive resources available on the Internet, I've selected a relatively small number that I think are the most important and valuable. There are also occasional references to other websites throughout this book. Be aware, of course, that websites come and go. These should be around for the foreseeable future, and I've checked them as late in the editing process of this book as possible, but some may have changed or vanished.

### News about testing

These are some valuable resources for an ongoing look at testing events and issues nationwide, as well as a resource for researching recent coverage. All have excellent search capacities. Most local newspapers also have searchable websites.

*Education Week* (http://www.edweek.org)
This weekly newspaper of education, focusing on K–12 schools, has frequent coverage of testing and standards. *Education Week* is also an active player through its annual "Quality Counts" assessment of states' participation in the standards agenda. The site's free searchable archive goes back to 1981.

*New York Times* (http://www.nytimes.com)
This site is a good source of solid reporting and some opinion pieces about standards and testing in a national context. Although some of the articles focus on New York, the *Times* is a national newspaper that covers all important testing and standards stories nationwide (use the "search" function). Richard Rothstein's intelligent weekly education column "Lessons" (on Wednesdays) often addresses issues of testing and standards. Articles published in the previous week are available for free, but articles from the archives now unfortunately cost up to $2.50 each to retrieve.

*National Education Writers Association* (http://www.ewa.org)
This national organization of education journalists includes links to articles on various topics such as testing and school reform, primarily from newspapers around the country. It's an excellent way to get a sense of what's currently attracting the attention of the public about testing and other educational topics in many locations. There are also links to recent research reports and a variety of education-related websites.

### Advocacy sites

These are, I believe, among the most important individuals and groups dealing with testing issues, and they all provide links to other sites.

*Alfie Kohn* (http://www.alfiekohn.org)
Kohn, a widely recognized author on testing and other topics, provides resources for those interested in opposing the excesses of standardized testing. Kohn includes a great deal of background information and evidence against a narrow standards movement, including many of his own articles.

*Gerald Bracey* (http://www.america-tomorrow.com/bracey)
Gerald Bracey is an important researcher of and commentator on American education. (See References.) If you follow the link here to sign up for EDDRA, you'll be able to visit Bracey's Education Disinformation Detection and Reporting Agency, including his many lively articles critiquing school-bashing and the excesses of the standards movement. You'll also receive periodic email updates.

*FairTest* (http://www.fairtest.org)
The National Center for Fair and Open Testing (FairTest) is the major advocacy group focusing on issues of standardized testing. Its website is a rich source for data, articles, political information, news stories, and publications on testing, as well as a list of state coordinators for advocacy on testing issues. They also sponsor the Assessment Resource Network (ARN) listserv, an important source of current activity and contacts around the country. FairTest also publishes a quarterly newsletter as well as books and pamphlets, which can be ordered through the website.

### State testing sites

*The Florida Association of School Administrators* (http://www.fasa.net/states.html)
This site provides links to all the state department of education websites, where links to standards and testing information can usually be found. A complete listing of state testing sites can also be found in Harris (2000) and its companion books. Virginia's site (http://www.pen.k12.va.us/VDOE/Assessment/)

is an example of comprehensive public disclosure of standards, tests, procedures, and so on.

## knowing something versus answering test questions

**What it means:** Failure to pick the right multiple-choice answer on a test doesn't necessarily mean that you don't know anything about the subject.

**Example:** Test item: How long ago did dinosaurs live? [Choose one of four answers]; Knowledge assessed more broadly: What do you know about when dinosaurs lived?

### What you need to know about it

We periodically hear complaints about what our students don't know. For instance, Ravitch and Finn, in *What Do Our 17-Year-Olds Know?* (1988) used data from the National Assessment of Educational Progress to complain that 68 percent of students don't know, for instance, when the Civil War took place: "We would contend that it is impossible to understand American history at all if one lacks any idea of when the Civil War occurred. It is not only the single most traumatic and decisive domestic event since the thirteen colonies won their independence from Britain; it is also the anchoring event of the nineteenth century, the climactic conflict to which other major events led and from which many others resulted" (50).

However, more precisely, the data tell us something slightly different: that 68 percent of seventeen-year-olds answered the following multiple-choice question (Ravitch and Finn 1988, 49) incorrectly:

When was the Civil War?
___ Before 1750        3.7%
___ 1750–1800         22.6

| | |
|---|---|
| ___ 1800–1850 | 38.4 |
| ___ 1850–1900 | 32.2 (correct answer) |
| ___ 1900–1950 | 2.5 |
| ___ After 1950 | 0.6 |

A quibble, you may say, but not necessarily. The most common incorrect answer doesn't look so horrifying in the context of the question as a whole (which Ravitch and Finn at least have the integrity to include). Also, there may be other reasons for getting the question wrong, such as carelessness or not putting a lot of energy into a test whose results don't impact you personally. I'm not trying to rationalize the students' performance but merely to point out that this measure is somewhat removed from a more direct assessment of student knowledge about when the Civil War occurred, such as having a conversation with a student about it. (By the way, for historical perspective, Rothstein [1998, 15] points out that in 1943 the *New York Times* discovered that only 29 percent of college freshmen knew that St. Louis is located on the Mississippi and only 6 percent could name the original thirteen states. Outcries about how little students know aren't new!)

This equating of what students know with how they answer a test item has been around for years, but I recently came across some information that suggests that it's being taken to new heights with disturbing implications for teaching and learning.

Virginia's recent standards have been understandably not just criticized but mocked for seeming wildly inappropriate in their complexity. For instance, a third-grade standard is "The student will explain the term *civilization* and describe the ancient civilizations of Greece and Rome, in terms of geographic features, government, agriculture, architecture, music, art, religion, sports, and roles of men, women, and children." Curious about this, I visited Virginia's extensive testing website (http://www.pen.k12.va.us/VDOE/Instruction/sol.html) to see how the standard played out in practice.

When I looked up the curriculum guide for history and social science, rather than finding ideas for interesting explorations of Greek and Roman culture, I saw a brief definition of civilization and factoids about each element included in the standard (e.g., Greece: Parthenon; Rome: Coliseum, aqueducts).

The almost laughably ambitious goals identified in the standards, therefore, had become testable trivia when translated into curriculum. The released third-grade test items for 1998 included on the website included only two history questions; one was purely on the level of factual recall and suggests how narrowly specific the testing would be. (The other was an easy question about the difference between the 1800s and today.) (Due to copyright restrictions, I can't reprint the questions, but you can find them at http:// www.pen.k12.va.us/VDOE/Assessment/samptests/solsamp3.html [follow the link for Grade Three History]).

Therefore, the lofty standard that Virginia has set for what third-graders should learn about Greek and Roman history may have turned out in practice to be about preparing students for a test item like the following (my invention):

A famous piece of Greek architecture was:
(a) the Coliseum
(b) aqueducts
(c) the Parthenon
(d) the Pyramids

Although the state website does include some excellent curriculum resources (at http://www.pen.k12.va.us/VDOE/Instruction/wmstds), *The Washington Post* (Shaver 1997) reported that teachers in Virginia are feeling pressured into putting much of their energy into focusing on material that's likely to be included on the test:

> Some Virginia teachers have criticized the state's forthcoming tests as too factbased, saying they worry they will be forced to turn from creative teaching to more rote memorization. "It's

a tremendous amount of pressure coming from administrators saying, 'These students have got to pass, they have to pass,'" said Meg Gruber, president of the Prince William Education Association. "How do you ensure someone passes a certain test? You drill and drill and drill what you know is supposed to be on that test."

The state curriculum guides would make it very easy to drill students on a series of undigested facts and generalizations about culture, rather than truly learning about it.

## Lake Wobegon effect

**What it means:** Everyone's above average.

**Example:** We're all richer, smarter, and cooler than the average person. (Don't we wish?)

### What you need to know about it

In 1987, John J. Cannell, a West Virginia physician, made headlines with his discovery that every state in the country had reported that their students scored above average on standardized tests (Cannell 1988, 1989). He dubbed this the "Lake Wobegon effect," after Garrison Keillor's mythical community where "the men are good-looking, the women are strong, and all the children are above average."

Cannell's report was followed up by further analyses (see Haney, Madaus, and Lyons 1993 for an overview), but the basic truth remained: that a seeming statistical impossibility was being achieved. Here's how it plays out: A test is developed and norms established so that you can determine how any given test taker compares to other test takers. Almost always, though, you're *not* compared to everyone else taking the test at the same time. If that were true, half the scores would always be below average and half above (by definition). However, the comparison is actually to the group to which the test was originally normed (developed).

There are a number of reasons why more than half of a group could score above average: If a test was developed in 1992, students taking it in 2002 might know more than students did in 1992. This is all well and good, but it's misleading to say that one particular group of those students is above average when they're merely above what the average was in 1992; it says nothing about how they stack up against other students today.

There are also, of course, less benign explanations. If a 1992 test was used in a district for ten years, the curriculum might have been gradually changed to be a better match to the test. The above average scores are then a bit of a fib, since the test was presumably normed on students studying all kinds of curriculum, not just those that fit the test (Haney et al. 1993). Even test familiarity makes a difference, since scores will often drop when a new test is introduced.

It's easy to imagine that the Lake Wobegon effect could have arisen quite innocently, with education improving over time in every state and this improvement being mistaken, in every case, for better performance as compared to other students. (Then there would be, of course, a rude awakening when the test was renormed.) However, Cannell suggests that something a little more devious may also have been taking place. Posing as a superintendent, he contacted a testing company. A saleswoman implied that scores for the poor rural district whose name he used would be above average if they used one of the company's older tests, and that their scores would go up every year. Cannell wondered, of course, how she could know that their district would be above average, let alone that student learning would increase every year (Cannell 1989, as cited in Haney et al. 1993). Would it be too terribly cynical to suggest a scam based on some simple knowledge about outcomes when using tests based on older norms and re-using them every year?

Given the pressures to raise test scores, is this surprising? Reporting scores as grade equivalents can add to the pressure (see **Grade Level**). If a school system is scolded in the media because only 45 percent of students are reading at grade level or above, it sounds much worse than saying that 45 percent, rather than the expected 50 percent, are above the mean, but it means exactly the same thing. If we want the majority of students to be reading at grade level or above (if we use grade-level equivalent scores as the indication of this), it means we're asking that the majority be above average. This simply can't be true for every school, or even every state.

## The National Assessment of Educational Progress (NAEP)

**What it means:** A federal program that regularly tests students nationwide in reading, writing, mathematics, science, and other subjects.

**Example:** News headlines from the *New York Times*: "12th Graders' National Science Scores Slip" (November 21, 2001); "Gap between Best and Worst Widens on U.S. Reading Test" (April 7, 2001).

### What you need to know about it

The National Assessment of Education Progress began in 1967 as a result of a Congressional mandate (Sacks 1999). Even if you aren't familiar with the name of this organization, you've probably seen reports of its work in the media over the years. Periodic reports of "what our kids know" and "how our students are doing" in areas like reading, writing, math, and history, usually involving tests at ages 9, 13, and 17 and showing state-by-state comparisons, come from NAEP. A search of the *New York Times* and *Education Week* archives (see **Internet Resources**) showed frequent news stories reporting on its findings.

What's important about NAEP's work? First, it's the closest thing we have to a national test. Although not all states take part, most do, and the others are encouraged to by advocates such as

*Education Week*, which includes participation in NAEP as a criterion in its annual state education scorecard.

Second, NAEP has the resources to do a fairly good job of testing. For instance, the writing test asks students to write. The math test asks students to think on paper and write explanations, not just answer multiple-choice questions. Since it tests only a sample of students rather than all of them (which makes sense for a group assessment), NAEP can afford to assess and analyze its data in ways that are more labor-intensive and complex than machine-scored multiple-choice tests (although it also includes many of the latter). For instance, writing assessment includes trait assessments by raters on a number of dimensions, and the percentage of misspelled words and numbers of punctuation and capitalization errors are tabulated.

Third, since NAEP isn't tied to a particular curriculum model and since scores aren't reported for particular schools or districts but rather nationally and by state, there's no particular avenue or incentive for teaching to the test or cheating, ensuring that NAEP's tests provide a relatively pure measure. (In fact, each student is given a short test containing only a limited sample of a wide range of questions, making targeted teaching almost impossible [Rothstein 2001b].)

Fourth, NAEP provides data over time, as subject areas are retested every several years. Since a sample of all students is tested, the comparisons from one year to the next are far more meaningful than changes in a measure like scores on the SAT, which is taken by a self-selected group of the college-bound.

Fifth, NAEP has made large amounts of data widely available. Each set of findings is reported in a brief summary often called a "report card" (e.g., *NAEP 1998 Writing Report Card for the Nation and the States*, Donahue, et al. 1999), backed up by more detailed reports that include large quantities of data and analysis. All of this material is available on microfiche through the ERIC Document Reproduction Service (obtainable through libraries). One can also request free copies of any of the reports through the National Center for Education Statistics (http://www.nces.ed.gov/nationsreportcard/site/home.asp), where the most recent are also available for download.

This material is a valuable resource for scholars. For instance, Kenneth Goodman (1998) was disturbed when California's lowered reading scores on NAEP were used to make the blanket claim that "whole language caused California's reading scores to plummet." He discovered in the NAEP reports that the students of teachers who practiced whole-language techniques like the use of trade books for reading had higher reading scores than the teachers of students who followed more traditional practices like using basal readers exclusively.

Sixth, NAEP is a high-quality assessment that serves as a check on possibly less accurate state assessments. Monty Neill (*Talk of the Nation* 2000) has pointed out that there have been cases where student scores on state tests have risen (often to the accompaniment of much publicity) but the states' NAEP scores have dropped. According to Neill, many of the state tests are less well designed and measure lower-level knowledge. If scores have been improved by teaching to this kind of test, he posits, more complex learning may have decreased, leading to score declines on NAEP exams.

Given all these benefits of the NAEP assessments, they deserve to be more widely known and used. In particular, states that are planning to institute expensive and disruptive testing paraphernalia should be asked to justify what these tests do that NAEP isn't already doing.

## passing (cutoff) scores

*What it means:* A test score is used as an absolute cutoff rather than in conjunction with other information.

*Example:* If you got a score of 640 on the PRAXIS reading exam, you can become a reading specialist in Oregon. If not, you can't.

### What you need to know about it

When a test is used to make a decision about whether, for instance, you've passed or failed a grade or are allowed to get a teaching license, a particular score is set as a passing or cutoff score. Let's think about a simple situation of a classroom test and how a teacher might decide what a passing grade is. One choice would be a criterion-referenced one, to say that you've passed if you answered perhaps 60 percent of the questions correctly. (Finer gradations of this can be used to assign grades like A, B, and C.) However, if the test is a particularly hard one and even good students don't do well, they could justifiably complain that the passing score had been set unfairly or arbitrarily.

Okay, let's try it another way. You figure that about 90 percent of your students study for your tests and perform satisfactorily on them, so you grade on a curve, which in this case means setting a cutoff score at the point where 90 percent of the students pass and 10 percent fail, which compensates for a particular test's being easier or harder. But there's room for student complaint here as well. Rigging the system so that 10 percent always fail hardly seems fair or motivating.

If this discussion sounds familiar, it's because it's another example of the distinction between criterion-referenced and norm-referenced assessment, both of which can be problematic when differences in performance are divided into categories that are used to make high-stakes decisions.

Let's look at some examples from the real world. Virginia made the news when only 6.5 percent of its schools met the state's testing benchmarks in 1999 (Schrag 2000), even though many of the "failing" schools had large numbers of students who had done well on the rigorous Advanced Placement Tests that give college credit to high school students. Massachusetts recently instituted a much-criticized test for prospective teachers that many applicants failed, including some who were highly educated in their subject areas. In both of these cases, the passing score was clearly criterion-referenced but with an unrealistically high criterion (given other data about the quality of Virginia students and of Massachusetts teacher education students). Although it may seem that a criterion-referenced passing score can be set disinterestedly without reference to how many test-takers are likely to pass, these examples show how flawed and arbitrary this process can be.

So in practice, even criterion-referenced cutoff scores are typically adjusted to reflect the composition of the test-takers so that an acceptable proportion of them pass. What's an acceptable proportion? That depends. When there's a rhetoric of high standards, the bar is often set fairly high, but then we're faced with consequences like large numbers of students having to go to summer school. Politicians who are happy to have large numbers of students receive failing scores when they're criticizing the schools are likely to be less sanguine about high failure rates a few years later, after their own reforms have been put in place. And, as Rothstein (2001a) has pointed out, proposed federal requirements that students pass state tests are basically meaningless since states can define passing scores however they like.

Perhaps the problem is with setting passing scores in the first place. In the case of licensing professionals like lawyers and barbers, we need to protect the public from incompetence and perhaps a case can be made that there's a specific body of knowledge that they do indeed need to have mastered, but does a similar argument apply to fourth-graders? If a decision is made to retain a student, surely it should take into account a variety of factors such as maturity and emotional impact, particularly given how much we know about the negative effects of retention (e.g., Owings and Magliaro 1998). In areas such as teacher licensing or college admissions, one could perhaps argue that there's a certain, relatively low test score below which applicants are unlikely to be successful, but beyond that point it seems that it makes more sense to look at test scores as one piece of information rather than as a strict gatekeeper, as most college admissions offices indeed do.

I've found that in working with teacher education students in a state where passing scores for admission to our programs have been set quite high (by the state, not the university), every year we have a number of otherwise strong applicants who have scored just below the cutoff and spend a lot of time and energy studying to retake the test and in some cases following alternative routes like preparing a portfolio. Shouldn't the state leave it up to the university to assess these prospective teachers and let the students put their efforts into learning what they need to learn to be a good teacher, not jumping through the state's testing hoop?

In summary, when a passing score has been set for a test, I believe we have a right to ask not only why and how the cutoff score has been set at a particular point, but why a set passing score is being required in the first place.

## percentiles and stanines

**What it means:** How one person being measured compares to another.

**Example:** If you're in the 63rd percentile on a test, 37 percent of test-takers scored higher than you. If you're in the sixth stanine, you're a little above average.

### What you need to know about it

A percentile provides information about how a student's score on a norm-referenced test compares to that of other test-takers, and is probably the single most useful (and most used) indicator of such a score. It's easy to understand, but it's also important not to confuse it with similar terms like percentage.

A percentile score is a *rank*; if you scored in the 50th percentile this means (by definition) that you scored higher than half the test-takers (usually those that the test was normed on). The number 50 has nothing to do with how many or what percentage of the test items you got right. In tests that have been designed so that the scores of all test-takers produce a standard bell curve (also known as the normal curve), percentile ranks match up to scores in a consistent way. For instance, an IQ of 115 (15 points above the average of 100) is at the 83rd percentile and an IQ of 85 (15 points below the average) is at the 17th percentile; IQ scores have been set up in such a way that two-thirds of test-takers' scores (if drawn randomly from the population as a whole) will fall between 85 and 115. Similarly, SAT scores of 400 and 600 fall at the 17th and 83rd percentiles, respectively (although this is true in reference to the norming group, not each year's body of test-takers).

Remember that percentiles are ranks, which means that they can't be treated like percentages. If a student's percentile rank on a standardized test goes from 25 one year to 50 the next, we can't say that she's doing twice as well as before (let alone that she knows twice as much as before) or that her score has doubled. The percentile tells us only that she has now outperformed half of her fellow students where before she outperformed only a quarter of them.

Stanine scores are single digits from one to nine, similar to percentiles in that they indicate ranks but a little misleading since they aren't equal in size; for instance, stanine 5 includes not one-ninth but 20 percent of test-takers.

**Percentage of scores in each stanine**

| Stanine | 1 | 2 | 3 | 4 | 5 | 6 | 7 | 8 | 9 |
|---|---|---|---|---|---|---|---|---|---|
| Percent in stanine | 4 | 7 | 12 | 17 | 20 | 17 | 12 | 7 | 4 |

Stanines aren't used as much as they used to be, since they were developed in order to have a single-digit measure of rank in the early days of computers, when space on punch cards (are you old enough to remember those?) was at a premium (Bracey 2000b).

It's important to keep in mind that percentiles and stanines always indicate how well you did in comparison to others, not in relation to a criterion. As Bracey (2000b) points out, even the loser in an eight-person Olympic race is still the eighth-fastest person on the planet that day.

## politics of testing

**What it means:** Who decides.

**Example:** A new superintendent buys a new test package.

### What you need to know about it

In an educational context, I find it useful to think of a political issue as being one that has to do with who makes decisions about what goes on in classrooms. In a highly politicized educational climate, many people and organizations other than the teachers and students who spend time in those classrooms are involved in the decision-making process.

I don't wish to speculate on the intentions and goodwill of those involved in specific cases; however, I *would* like to raise some concerns about how educational practice can be affected by the interests and agendas of those making the decisions.

Remember that the whole point of test scores is to be an indicator of student learning and knowledge; they aren't an end in themselves. However, if they're seen in the public arena as the primary indicator of educational quality, they will become an end in themselves—not only for the unscrupulous and manipulative, but for those sincerely concerned with the welfare of students who nonetheless lose sight of the real goal.

Let's take some hypothetical examples. If you're a politician whose constituency is wealthier families, you can use low test scores to advocate for vouchers or for punitively taking funds away from low-scoring schools, typically found in poorer neighborhoods. If you're a politician from the party not in power, you may decide to say that test scores are too low and we need to do better. If you win the election, getting the scores to go up will be a major goal. The same is true if you're a principal, particularly if you're a new one who's been brought in to raise the scores of an underperforming school. In both cases, remember that raising the scores and improving education are not necessarily accomplished by the same means. In particular, there are a variety of ways to improve scores without improving learning. (See **Ethics**.)

One way to make scores go up is to retain students. If low-performing fourth-graders are passed to fifth grade, they'll bring a school's scores down more there than they would if they stayed in fourth grade for another year (since they'd be further behind the other students in their class). Given these circumstances, can we be sure that when students are being retained, it's always in their best interest? In high school, low-scoring students are sometimes among the more disruptive ones; a strict discipline policy with a lot of expulsions can therefore raise your test scores because of whom it weeds out.

If you're in a state where the newspapers print the percentage of students per school that reached the state benchmark, your educational goals may shift, seemingly slightly but actually significantly, from helping all students learn to increasing the number of students meeting the benchmark. In Oregon, there have been stories of educational triage, where teachers are encouraged not to worry about the students who are already meeting the benchmark or those who have little chance of doing so but rather to put the bulk of their energy into working with the students who are just below benchmark level.

I could go on, but you get the idea. Even if everyone in the system were operating with full integrity, it would still be easy to put policies in place that have the result of raising test scores but with other, unintended but negative, consequences. In every case where a decision is made that could have an impact on test scores, therefore, let's look carefully at what the consequences are to the decision-maker (including classroom teachers) if scores go up or down. If there's a vested interest involved, these decisions should be carefully scrutinized.

## professional organizations

**What it means:** Organizations that are made up of teachers and scholars, and that publish journals, hold conferences, and work to develop and generally define best practice in their field.

**Example:** International Reading Association, National Council for the Social Studies, National Association for the Education of Young Children, Council for Exceptional Children, and many others.

### What you need to know about it

Around 1993, the National Council of Teachers of English (NCTE) and the International Reading Association (IRA) began working on an ambitious series of standards for the English Language Arts for grades K–12, funded by a contract from the U.S. Department of Education. In 1994, the government decided not to continue funding the project since it felt the results so far were too vague and failed to "define what students should know and be able to do," nor did the project attempt to set a list of what books all students should read, or take a stand on standard versus invented spelling (Diegmueller 1994). This action was greeted with a great deal of attention and shock, although some observers (such as Shannon 1996) regretted that IRA and NCTE had gotten involved in the project in the first place.

The two professional associations continued their work, however, funding it themselves and producing not only a list of standards but a variety of publications designed to help teachers put them into practice. (These materials can be ordered through either organization: Their websites are http://www.ncte.org and http://www.reading.org. The standards themselves and related material are available online at the NCTE site.) Other professional organizations in the field of education, beginning with the National Council of Teachers of Mathematics (NCTM), have developed similar standards and accompanying curricula.

The English language arts standards, like others (see Nash, Crabtree, and Dunn 1997, for instance, for a recounting of the story of the history standards) weren't received entirely favorably by the public and the media. The IRA/NCTE standards were accused of being vague and full of jargon. However, they're viewed generally (although not unanimously) favorably within the profession, and are seen as providing guidance to teachers about what's important (particularly through the accompanying curriculum materials) and as lending credence to particular practices by giving them the imprimatur of the experts in the field. The standards also recognize the importance of a variety of approaches and don't advocate some programs and techniques to the exclusion of others, nor do they endorse commercial programs.

Although there are likely to be disagreements among professionals about some of the details of standards like the English language arts ones and others, what's important about them is that they represent the current best thinking of a broad consensus of the profession. They were developed out of the thinking of large numbers of teachers, academics, and other authorities in the field. It would seem logical that when states developed their own standards, they'd want to draw on this national expertise.

Well, this isn't what happened. As state departments of education began to develop standards for reading and language arts, we didn't hear how they'd drawn on national standards developed by the professional organizations. And indeed, what they developed looked very different. Here are some examples of how the IRA/NCTE standards contrasted with those from Oregon and Virginia:

| IRA/NCTE (K–12) | Virginia (Third grade) | Oregon (Fifth grade benchmark) |
|---|---|---|
| 4. Students adjust their use of spoken, written, and visual language (e.g., conventions, style, vocabulary) to communicate effectively with a variety of audiences and for different purposes. 5. Students employ a wide range of strategies as they write.... 6. Students apply knowledge of language structure, language conventions (e.g., spelling and punctuation), media techniques, figurative language, and genre to create, critique, and discuss print and nonprint texts. | 3.7: The student descriptive paragraphs. a) Develop a plan for writing. b) Focus on a central idea. c) Group related ideas. | Structure writing by developing a beginning, middle, and end with clear sequencing of ideas and transitions. Students will: • develop a recognizable beginning that introduces the audience to the topic. • develop a clearly sequenced body that contains identification of main topics and supporting details about the topics • develop a conclusion • use some transitional words (e.g., first, then, finally, also) |

As you can see, the standards developed by a wide range of English language arts professionals are broadly focused, with an emphasis on communication, purpose, and variety, while the state standards are much more narrowly outcome-oriented with traditional goals. Why the disjunction? My guess is that it's basically political in nature. The goal of the professional organizations was primarily to develop standards representing current thinking about best practice in the field; the way they went about this task ensured that a wide range of viewpoints was taken into account. Although states undoubtedly vary in how their standards have been developed and by whom, the form that they so often end up taking suggests that their goals are not just (or perhaps even primarily) about best practice but include considerations of what's measurable and what the public and elected officials would like to see the standards include.

Doesn't the public have a right to set the aims of education? Sure, but doesn't it also have a responsibility to listen to those who have devoted their careers to developing expertise in the field? Imagine a state medical board's setting standards for practice without consulting with the American College of Physicians and Surgeons.

In the process, IRA and NCTE have been not only ignored but sometimes vilified. An editorial in the Indianapolis *Star* ("Truth About Reading" 2000); where the IRA was having its annual convention, characterized the IRA as a whole-language organization that willfully neglected phonics as promoted by the recent report of the National Reading Panel. (Timothy Shanahan [2000], the chair of the National Reading Panel, wrote a letter to the newspaper to correct the editorial's many misconceptions.) A professional organization was thus written off as the pawn of one side of a (somewhat mythical) debate about practice; this stance can then be used as a justification for not drawing on its work. It's the students, of course, who suffer in the end from not being educated according to the best thinking in the profession.

## reading comprehension assessment

**What it means:** Evaluating whether a student has understood what she's read.

**Example:** Depending on whom you ask, a discussion with the reader or a multiple-choice question.

### *What you need to know about it*

Reading comprehension can be instructive to examine as an example of what seems to be a pretty large gap between what tests claim to measure and what they actually do measure. I think we'd all agree that it's important for students to be able to read material of an appropriate difficulty and understand it. In classroom practice this might involve being able to participate intelligently in a group discussion of a book, or write an interesting response to it. On a more exalted level, countless books of literary theory have been written exploring one or another understanding of Proust or Faulkner, or the ways that readers come to comprehend and interpret literature in general.

Diagnostically, techniques such as miscue analysis (Wilde 2000) get at comprehension through interactions with a reader that encourage her to retell what she's read in her own words, followed by probing questions that attempt to mine knowledge that hasn't surfaced on its own. The teacher may then use a scoring guide that assesses how completely and accurately the reader has understood the text.

Now let's go to a typical multiple-choice reading comprehension test. An excerpt from *Charlotte's Web* might be followed by questions such as the following (my invention):

1. What kind of animal was Wilbur?
   a. beaver
   b. pig
   c. goose
   d. hedgehog

2. What's the *best* statement of what Charlotte taught Wilbur?
   a. You can always count on your friends.
   b. Life on the farm is hard.
   c. We still have memories of those who have died.
   d. You can get along with those who are different from you.

Okay, this is a bit of a parody but there's indeed quite a gap between what reading comprehension looks like in everyday life in the classroom (and indeed, in our own lives as readers) and how it ends up being measured on tests. (Or at least I thought it was a parody until I discovered, thanks to Susan Ohanian [2000], a website developed by Sylvan Learning Centers [http://www.BookAdventure.org] where kids can test themselves after reading a book with some of the most vapid comprehension questions I've seen.)

There are at least two concerns about this reductionism. First, is it necessarily reading comprehension that's being measured? As Deborah Meier (1981) has pointed out, children's thinking processes may lead them to pick an answer other than the "correct" one, but this doesn't necessarily mean that they weren't able to understand what they read. Instead, it is perhaps an indication of their background knowledge, maturity in thinking, and so on. When Meier asked children how they came up with their (wrong) answers, their responses often seemed reasonable and logical, although it was typically a child's logic. (Meier also discovered that reading the items aloud to the children didn't make a difference; she wondered, therefore, if reading was what was really being tested.) Hill and Larsen (2000) have written a book-length report on similar material. (See **Essential Resources**.)

Those who do best on this kind of test are often those who have understood what they've read *and* are good at understanding the way testmakers frame their questions. Although children who read well are likely to do well on reading comprehension tests and those who don't are not (obviously someone who couldn't read a story at all isn't likely to be able to answer comprehension questions about it), there's a significant risk of false negatives: students who understand what they read but don't score well on comprehension tests. If a standardized test were used merely as an initial screening device, or for a test like NAEP where such errors balance out across large groups, this wouldn't be a big concern. But once a test is used for a decision about an individual, such as placement in a reading group or retention in grade, we must be scrupulous about the accuracy of the assessment.

The other concern is the relationship between the test's format and the curriculum. If testing were kept separate from curriculum and used merely as a snapshot of student knowledge, then educators would be relatively free to develop curriculum according to best thinking in the field.

However, perhaps particularly in a standards-based approach, the form of measurement that's being planned can end up driving the curriculum. Thus when reading tests are designed to get at a series of defined "skills," it may well result in standards for reading being set in the form of a scope and sequence of specifics, often written in behavioral terms.

Here's an example. Literary elements like character, plot, setting, and theme are obvious features to examine when exploring literature with children. If I were teaching elementary school, I'd certainly be inviting students to look for passages where an author helps us understand what a particular character is like (for instance, the classic description of a typical day in the life of Wilbur the pig in *Charlotte's Web*). I'd also want to get them thinking about the meaning of what they've read. One example would be Natalie Babbitt's *Tuck Everlasting*, which prompts readers to think about why it might not be advantageous to live forever. Since this isn't a real-life choice (the book is fantasy, after all), it also encourages us to think about how authors use unusual or impossible plots to get us to think about our own more mundane lives.

These two children's classics could also lead to interesting discussions about different kinds of fiction: unlike realistic novels like Mildred Taylor's, neither *Charlotte's Web* or *Tuck Everlasting* could really happen, but they're different kinds of nonrealistic genres, an animal story and light fantasy, respectively. Mildred Taylor's novels set in the first half of the twentieth century are in a sense historical, but not in the same way as *Ben and Me*, a historical novel about Benjamin Franklin told by his pet mouse. Classroom explorations along these lines would obviously encourage high levels of reading comprehension, where students are encouraged not just to remember details of what they've read but to relate their reading to their own lives and also to other literature and, in a sense, to theories of literature and how it creates its effects.

Okay, let's come back to earth—with a bit of a thud, perhaps. Here are two examples of benchmarks from Oregon standards, along with relevant sample test items (Oregon Department of Education 1999).

> Third grade: Students will identify main and supporting characters.
> Item from sample third-grade test, following an excerpt from *Sadako and the Thousand Paper Cranes*:
>
>> Which sentence below is true about the characters in this story?
>> A. Nurse Yasunaga is the main character.
>> B. Sadako and Chizuko are the main characters.
>> C. Sadako's mother is the main character.
>> D. This story doesn't have any main characters.[4]
>
> Fifth grade: Students will identify whether a passage is from a story, poem, play, or a nonfiction selection; students will identify characteristics representative of a given form.
> Item from sample fifth-grade test, following an excerpt from *Sarah, Plain and Tall*:
>
>> This story is fiction. We can say that because
>> A. the author made up the characters.
>> B. the characters don't act like real people.
>> C. it is about an important time in our country's history.
>> D. readers have to use imagination to see the scenery.

4. Although B is the correct answer for the excerpt on the test, readers who are familiar with the book might be confused since Sadako is clearly its main character and Chizuko a secondary one.

What's being assessed here are aspects of reading comprehension that are broader and more extensive than just whether you've understood the story you read, yet in the move from literary understandings to benchmarks to test items, they've become trivialized and diminished. It wouldn't be so harmful if the test just dropped out of the sky once a year, but Oregon's teachers have gotten the very clear message (in the form of a thick notebook and other materials) that these are the standards that they are responsible for and the ways that the students will be assessed on them. (In all fairness, it should be noted that Oregon's assessment also includes having students write responses to literature, which is a relative rarity in state testing.) It's only understandable that teachers would be more likely to focus on meeting the benchmarks than on richer approaches to reading comprehension, particularly when the former is the focus of inservice workshops, state and local conferences, and so on.

Arthur Wise (1979) has referred to the "hyperrationalization" of learning, where knowledge is assumed to be reducible to small pieces that can then be taught and tested. In the case of a complex process (not really a "skill") like understanding what you've read, this risks neglecting educators' stated goals in favor of manipulating terminology and designing instruction to mimic test items. If you think about your own reading comprehension, what it consists of, how it develops, and so on, it's complex, subtle, and the result of rich experiences with reading. You may well be able to answer reading comprehension test items with a good deal of success, but practicing answering comprehension questions isn't how you got to that point as a reader.

## reliability

**What it means:** Will scores derived from the same data be consistent?

**Example:** If a student takes the SAT twice, will his two scores be similar? Are two readers likely to assign the same holistic score to a piece of writing?

## What you need to know about it

Reliability is one of the two cornerstones of accuracy in testing and measurement (see **Validity** for the other). Put simply, will the same measurement give the same results for the same data every time? It's not just synonymous with accuracy. For instance, you might be able to live with your bathroom scale's being off by a few pounds, but you'd want it to be so consistently. If it weighed you two pounds light one day and four pounds heavy the next, you couldn't rely on it at all.

Reliability comes into play with educational testing since we realize that tests are only an indication of underlying knowledge, not a direct measure of it. We know, therefore, that a rater's assessment of a piece of writing isn't an exact science, but we also know that if a number of raters give similar scores to multiple pieces of writing, the system has some degree of meaningfulness.

Here are some typical examples of reliability in educational contexts. The scoring of multiple-choice tests is obviously very reliable at one level. Two teachers marking the same set of answer sheets are going to get the same results, barring a small degree of human error. Machine scoring is even more reliable. (This is why these tests are called objective; there may be a lot of subjectivity in the test writer's *deciding* which answer is the right one, but given an answer key, the scoring itself doesn't require any judgment.)

However, there's another important level of reliability as well. If Version A of a test like the SAT was appreciably easier than Version B, your score would vary according to which one you happened to get, and the SAT as a whole would therefore be lacking in reliability. (Reliability is a central reason why formal tests like the SAT are given as much as possible under the same conditions every time; see **Standardized**.) If you take a standardized test more than once (almost certainly getting a different version each time), it's unlikely you'd get exactly the same score, but for the test to be reliable your scores would need to fall within a relatively small range. Your "true" score is likely to fall somewhere in the middle of the range of the scores you got all the times that you took the test. If the test is more rather than less reliable, the individual scores will vary less widely.

Most long-established standardized tests have high reliability, in that scores are likely to be similar for someone taking the test in different versions. (Reliability is measured from zero, meaning that all differences in scores are due to measurement error, to 1.0, meaning that there is no difference at all in results from two versions of the test.) A reasonable level of test reliability is 0.85 or above (Bracey 2000b).

With states developing so many of their own tests, teachers and parents should be asking about their reliability. Is last year's test comparable to this year's? Reliability is, of course, particularly important when test scores are used to make decisions about individual students. Here's an example (in this case, a relatively benign one): The daughter of a friend of mine was eliminated from a special math program when the funding for it dropped and the numbers had to be reduced. Only those students with the highest standardized test scores in math were retained in the program. Aside from issues of whether this was the best criterion, it didn't account for the fact that some of the students falling below the cutoff might well have scored above it if given a retake. (Unfortunately, too, in this case the students retained in the program were mostly boys.)

Reliability is far harder to come by on tasks other than multiple-choice tests. To increase reliability on the scoring of material such as writing samples, states use procedures such as rubrics and rater training sessions. Typically, before working on real papers, judges will rate and then discuss their ratings for a set of practice papers until they're consistent in their scoring. Even so, it's hard to maintain reliability in this kind of scoring, and increased reliability often comes at the cost of a narrowed task or more controlled criteria for assessment. Scoring reliability and task authenticity thus tend to be mutually contradictory to some extent. The more your students write in ways that reflect the variety of real writing that they do, the harder their writing will be to score reliably. And since large-scale assessment is useless without reliability (since the scores can't be depended on without it), large-scale assessment of something like writing is unlikely to be very genuine.

## SAT tests

**What it means:** The most widely-used college admissions test in the United States, administered by the Educational Testing Service.

### What you need to know about it

Entire books have been written on the SAT tests (Lemann [1999] is the most recent), but I'd like to make just one point here about what they were designed for and, in contrast, what they're not meant to do.

Several years ago, the College Board, which sponsors the SAT exams administered by the Educational Testing Service, renormed the exams so that test-takers would be compared to their 1990 peers, rather than the original group that the scores were based on in 1941. (This discussion refers to what is now known as the SAT-I, the verbal and math test.) A student close to the average, who'd received a 428 (on a 200–800 scale) on the verbal test the year before would now get a score of 505. Educational historian Diane Ravitch made the following comments in an op-ed piece entitled "Defining Literacy Downward" in the *New York Times*:

> The College Board has turned the deplorable performance on the verbal test into a new norm. The old average was a standard that American education aspired to meet; the new average validates mediocrity.

The College Board maintains that colleges know that a 500 on the verbal exam is the equivalent of a 430 on the old scale, that the test is just as hard as it used to be, and that it still ranks students in the same order.

But do students and parents know that they received bonus points for good timing rather than better performance? Does the public understand that the higher scores are the result of statistical legerdemain?

By readjusting the norms, the American education deficit seems to have been eliminated. But nothing has changed, other than the loss of a high and unwavering standard. (Ravitch 1996)

Ravitch's comments reflect a persistent misunderstanding about the purpose and legitimate uses of the SAT test.

These tests, formerly known as the Scholastic Aptitude and then the Scholastic Assessment Tests but now just called the SAT-I, are designed to help colleges make admission decisions by predicting first-year college success (i.e., grade-point averages). Sophisticated admissions officers use them as one criterion, to be looked at in the context of grades, recommendations, and so on. (The subject-area tests of the SAT-II provide more specific information about content learning.) Information about the average SAT scores of entering freshmen at individual colleges is widely available and can give applicants a sense of whether they are likely to get into a particular school and whether it would be a good match for them.

Given these purposes, it makes sense that a 500 score should be the average score for current test-takers. The score distribution for all students taking the test is then a good match with the bell curve that the range of scores is designed to represent. Admissions offices can then know that the easily-remembered score points of 500, 600, 700, and 800 represent the 50th, 84th, 98th, and 99.9th percentiles, respectively, in relation to today's population of college applicants.

What's Ravitch's glaring misconception? She seems to believe that the College Board is cheating by making it look like students are doing better than they really are. But the SATs were never meant to tell us how well our students are doing in general, and can never do so. Unfortunately, every year the College Board releases statistics about SAT scores that are then subject to media commentary, reinforcing the impression that they provide us with an annual snapshot of our high school graduates.

Here's the problem. (These points have been discussed at length by a number of scholars, including Berliner and Biddle 1995; Bracey 1997; and Sacks 1999.) Students who take the SAT exam are a self-selected group, not a representative group. Therefore, their scores don't tell us anything about American high school students as a whole and never will.

For one thing, SAT test-takers in 1941 were an elite, largely white male group. As college attendance has become more common, a far wider cross-section of students began to take the SATs, so scores understandably dropped over the years. Comparing one state's SAT scores to another' is also misleading. (The College Board knows such comparisons are inappropriate, but doesn't actively discourage them [Lavergne 2001].) In some states, the state colleges require SATs, while other states rely on another test, the ACT. SAT scores in those ACT states—like Iowa—tend to be high, since the SATs are taken there primarily by students going to out-of-state colleges, who are likely to be stronger students than those staying in-state.

Here's another wrinkle: Imagine a cynical politician who wanted to take credit for higher SAT scores on his watch. One way to do so would be to drastically curtail federal financial aid programs like Pell Grants (which was done in the Reagan administration). Statistically, students from lower-income families (that is, those most in need of such grants) tend to score lower. Eliminating them from the SAT pool by eliminating their financial ability to go to college would raise scores overall.

As Richard Rothstein (2000) has pointed out, sophisticated analysis of SAT scores can give us useful information about trends. For instance, he suggested that since African-American students taking the SAT (and the similar ACT) are a greater proportion of all black 18-year-olds than was the case in 1976, but their average scores have risen nonetheless, this is an encouraging sign of progress. But SAT scores will never be a good quick indicator of how our schools and students are doing; the annual pontificating that usually accompanies the release of the scores is basically meaningless since it's using the data inappropriately.

## spelling assessment (as an exemplar of broader issues)

**What it means:** How well kids spell.

**Example:** It depends on what exactly we want to know.

### What you need to know about it

I'd like to use the topic of spelling to illustrate many of the issues surrounding standards and assessment, not because it's particularly important to assess but because it's a topic that's relatively easy to get a handle on. A similar analysis could be done for other subject areas.

Let's start with a broad goal for spelling instruction: that most students should, by the end of elementary school, be able to produce a piece of writing with most of the words spelled correctly, using a variety of resources including dictionaries and spell-checkers as well as a knowledge base of many known spellings, particularly of common words. I believe everyone—both educators and parents—is likely to agree with this goal. A sophisticated language arts teacher also knows that some students will reach this goal by third grade or so, and that for others, particularly those with learning disabilities, it'll be out of reach though still worth working toward. She also knows that spelling comes more easily to some students than others, and that those who struggle with spelling will have to work harder on editing their final drafts. Put in these terms, a standard for spelling seems relatively easy to define. And even if it isn't necessarily easy for all students to meet this standard, the teacher's job seems relatively obvious and manageable.

How would the teacher assess spelling in the classroom? The most useful evaluation tool would be the one that fits most closely with the instructional goal: children's ability to spell correctly in what they write. In the earlier grades, the teacher will be looking for an increasing ability to spell the most common words correctly; as students get older, she'll want to make sure they know how to find and fix their invented spellings and will set a higher standard for spelling in final drafts, though one still influenced by knowledge of individual differences between students. This classroom evaluation is also a diagnostic evaluation; if the teacher notices that Jimmy is still spelling *they* as *thay* in fourth grade, or that Tina takes forever to find a word in the dictionary, she'll introduce appropriate instruction.

Large-scale spelling assessment has typically been very different from this. The typical multiple-choice test of spelling includes four choices: usually either four spellings of the same word, from which the correct one is chosen, or four different words, from which the one that's spelled wrong is chosen. This is, of course, unconnected to spelling in real life, which is about producing spellings, not recognizing them. These tests do, however, correlate highly with tests of word dictation, so that they provide a much more efficient way of finding out how you would do if you were given these words to spell. However, what would it tell us if we were to dictate a spelling list to students?

First, is he familiar with this particular word (since few spellings are regular enough to predict just from pronunciation)? Second, does he have the kind of natural spelling ability that enables him to retain words once he's seen them in print? Neither of these questions seems very informative to evaluate, since the first is just a measure of general literacy development and the second has to do with your native capacity. Neither has much to do with what you're learning about spelling in school. (Even if you studied spelling words every week, it's unlikely that they'd be the words on the standardized test, unless the teacher was unethically teaching to the test.)

What should we be doing, then, if we want to see how our schools are doing in teaching spelling, and can we use a large-scale test to assess individuals? The method used by the National Assessment of Educational Progress, which involves determining the percentage of misspelled words in a writing sample (Campbell et al. 1996), comes the closest to being a good measure since it involves seeing how students actually do with spelling in their writing. It also provides the public with readily understandable information: For instance, in 1994, the proportion of misspelled words in a writing sample ranged from 9 percent for nine-year-olds to 3 percent for seventeen-year-olds. Not only is this more meaningful than a standardized test score, it shows that our students are doing pretty well in spelling.

Second best might be the approach taken by Oregon, where student writing is evaluated by analytic trait scoring, with one of the traits measured being conventions, including spelling. On the Oregon Department of Education's website where sample papers have been scored (http://beta.open.k12.or.us/scoring), the descriptions of the different scores for conventions seem to have resulted in a reasonable relationship between score and percentage of misspellings. (A score of six is described as demonstrating "exceptionally strong control of writing conventions . . . correct spelling, even of more difficult words," while a one indicates "frequent spelling errors that significantly impair readability.") The final overall results, however, are less informative to the public than NAEP's are, since they're folded into a single score for writing, in which students are then judged to have met a benchmark or not. (Conventions make up 40 percent of the composite score.)

Both NAEP and a system like Oregon's seem to offer a reasonable way to communicate to the public about how our schools are helping students learn to spell (although both are of course very expensive and labor-intensive). But what about individuals? A single piece of writing can't possibly provide adequate information about an individual's spelling. Also, a brilliant writer for whom spelling doesn't come easily could fail to meet the benchmark for writing in Oregon, even if that writer has made great strides in learning how to proofread his work.

In addition, if a student isn't doing well in spelling, it could indicate a number of very different situations: He might be lagging in literacy generally and hasn't read enough to be a good speller; she might be a strong reader and writer without a lot of natural spelling ability; he might never have learned how to proofread his writing; she might be unconcerned about spelling and unwilling to take the time to get it right. Each of these needs to be dealt with differently. When it comes right down to what we really need to know to help particular students achieve and seeing whether they've done so, there's no substitute for the informed teacher. A single test, even a relatively authentic one, can never be more than a rough indicator of any individual student's knowledge. If all these concerns are relevant, even with a fairly simple domain of knowledge like spelling, they are bound to be even more complex across other curriculum areas.

## standard deviation

**What it means:** How much variation there is in a group, also used to describe how much someone differs from the average.

**Example:** A random group of adults whose height averages 5'8" will have a much bigger standard deviation than a group of Radio City Rockettes, whose average height of about 5'8" represents a range only from 5'6" to 5'10".

### What you need to know about it

Imagine a group of seven friends with an average (mean) income of $30,000. The following are three possible configurations of each one's income.

| Equal incomes | | Similar incomes | | Different incomes | |
|---|---|---|---|---|---|
| Alice | 30K | Alice | 36K | Alice | 90K |
| Brian | 30K | Brian | 34K | Brian | 90K |
| Carol | 30K | Carol | 32K | Carol | 6K |
| Diego | 30K | Diego | 30K | Diego | 6K |
| Ellen | 30K | Ellen | 28K | Ellen | 6K |
| Frank | 30K | Frank | 26K | Frank | 6K |
| Grace | 30K | Grace | 24K | Grace | 6K |

These are obviously very different from each other; the friendships
in the first group, where everyone could afford similar restaurants,
would be very different from those in the third group where Alice
and Brian would want to eat at the Ritz while for everyone else
McDonald's would be a rare treat.

You can imagine a similar range with test scores. Let's say
you've taught a math unit and the mean score of your students on
the test you designed is 80 percent. You'd certainly want to know
which of the following configurations it represented:

| Similar scores | | Varied scores | |
|---|---|---|---|
| Harry | 83% | Harry | 100% |
| Isoke | 82% | Isoke | 100% |
| Jaime | 81% | Jaime | 100% |
| Kerry | 80% | Kerry | 100% |
| Larry | 79% | Larry | 100% |
| Maria | 78% | Maria | 30% |
| Nigel | 77% | Nigel | 30% |

The standard deviation is the statistic that tells you how much variation
went into a group's average score. It's determined by a statistical formula
that is easily carried out through a spreadsheet program. (The exact formula can be found in any statistics book.) Put simply, the standard deviation tells you how far away a typical score is from the average score.

Let's see how it works. For the income chart for the seven friends, in every case the mean is $30,000, but the standard deviations are 0, 4, and 37.9 (thousand dollars). This reflects that the first group's incomes are all the same, the second group's vary a little, and the third group's are very different. Similarly, for the test score chart, the standard deviations are 2 and 31.6.

Some widely used test scores like those of the SAT and Stanford-Binet IQ tests are calibrated so that test-takers' scores fit into a so-called normal curve, also known as the bell curve. In a bell curve, standard deviations always fall (by definition) at particular points and carry the same meaning.

Here's how it works. IQ tests have a mean of 100 and a standard deviation of 15. The SAT test has a mean of 500 and a standard deviation of 100. (In both cases, this applies to the group on which the test was normed, not necessarily any current group of test-takers.) In a normal curve, 68 percent of the scores fall within one standard deviation of the mean, 95 percent fall within two standard deviations, and 99.7 percent fall within three. On the IQ and SAT tests, then, it's easy to determine where in the population a particular score falls. (See also **Percentiles**.)

| IQ | SAT | How many standard deviations from the mean? | Percentile |
|---|---|---|---|
| 145 | 800 | +3 | 99.9 |
| 130 | 700 | +2 | 98 |
| 115 | 600 | +1 | 84 |
| 100 | 500 | 0 | 50 |
| 85 | 400 | −1 | 16 |
| 70 | 300 | −2 | 2 |
| 55 | 200 | −3 | 0.1 |

Put another way, if the population currently taking an IQ test or the SAT exam is comparable to the group the test was normed on, about

two-thirds of them will receive scores between 85 and 115 and between 400 and 600, respectively. (It's in order to preserve this quality that the SAT was recently renormed; see **SAT Tests**.)

However, the results of many newly developed tests, such as
state tests, don't follow the normal curve, since it's much more involved and time-consuming to develop a test so that scores fall into
this distribution. But it's still important that we get a sense of how
wide a range the average represents. When scores are made available to the public, the average scores should always be accompanied
by an indication of the standard deviation. This is especially true if
the average represents a very large group like an entire school district. (The standard deviation should also, of course, be explained
in a way that's understandable to the majority of the public that
doesn't know the concept.) Providing a standard deviation reveals
the difference between a school or district where all students are
doing well and one where the strong success of some students could
hide the failure of the schools to educate others.

## standardized

**What it means:** For a test, developed appropriately and administered under consistent conditions.

**Example:** Enforcing time limits on a timed test for all test-takers.

**What you need to know about it**

What standardized tests lack in relevance to a particular classroom
and curriculum, they make up for in their ability to make comparisons across large numbers of test-takers. (See Hopkins 1998, chapter 14, for a good overview.) A good standardized test is one that
enables such a comparison because of two important factors: testing conditions are controlled so that they're the same for everyone,
and test questions are carefully generated, analyzed, tried out, and

revised, and norms developed, so that the test consistently ranks students accurately (on its own terms, of course, since there are many concerns about the validity of these tests).

Awareness of these two important dimensions—standard test conditions and a careful item- and norm-development process—can help us be aware of what are and are not reasonable criticisms of such tests. Here are some examples. (I'll be referring here to the classic standardized achievement tests such as the SAT-9, Iowa Test of Basic Skills, Metropolitan Achievement Tests, and so on. These are different from many state tests, which are often criterion-referenced and may not have been normed.)

### "Most of my kids don't have time to finish the test, so they feel frustrated."

The norms of many if not most standardized tests have been established under timed conditions; in fact, each section of a test may have its own time limit. The purpose of the test is to rank students in relation to each other; this is more accurately done both by limiting and standardizing the time allowed and by including enough questions that only the top students have time to answer all of them. If the test were short enough for all students to finish, it would create a ceiling effect that would make it harder to rank the better students in relation to each other. Students might feel better if they were told that many students indeed won't have time to finish the test; if they did, it would mean the test wasn't working very well and needed to be revised.

However, students with certain learning disabilities are a special case. Some learners, it's believed, just need more time to demonstrate what they do indeed know. Students who have been classified as having a learning disability can request extra time for some tests such as the SAT. (Unfortunately, there have been reports of unscrupulous psychologists, for a price, falsely certifying students as learning disabled to gain them more time on the SAT and increase their chances of acceptance at competitive colleges.)

But for most students, giving them extra time on a time-limited standardized test, even if done with the good intentions of helping them better demonstrate what they know, is cheating pure and simple. The scores are only valid if obtained under the specified standard conditions.

### "The test doesn't seem fair because it covers a lot of stuff my kids haven't studied."

Norm-referenced standardized tests aren't meant to reflect any one curriculum. A math test will be a closer fit to different schools' curriculums than a social studies test will, since the latter includes a lot of regional variations, but the test was normed on students from all kinds of classrooms and the scoring takes that into account. (The only exception would be if a test happened to be an *unusually* good or bad fit with a particular school's curriculum.)

This also relates to the timing of the curriculum during the year. Many elementary school teachers, following the layout of their math textbooks, teach geometry later in the school year. If tests are given in April, it may seem unfair to have geometry included on the test since it hasn't been taught yet. However, it's only unfair if the test was normed exclusively on students who'd already studied geometry that year. If many students study geometry in May, an April test will measure what they remember from the previous year. Moving geometry (or any topic) earlier in the year just because of the test distorts the results.

### "I need to use spelling textbooks and basal readers in fifth grade because the kids are going to be tested on the fifth-grade spelling words and reading skills."

This completely inaccurate but surprisingly common misconception results from a sense that there's a uniform curriculum out there, embodied in textbooks, that grows out of a master list of content for each grade. I first encountered it when a teacher at a spelling workshop felt she needed a spelling book in order to make sure the kids learned the words that would be on the standardized test for spelling for her grade. Our educational apparatus is, of course, nowhere near that unified. Although there's a certain degree of similarity across different textbook series, it's not at the level of specific spelling words or skill areas. But even more importantly, although test items need to reflect typical curricula in a general sense, individual items are included and excluded in part because they do a good job of ranking test-takers. Therefore, the words on a fifth-grade spelling test are not those that all fifth-graders should have learned but rather those that have been shown to be missed by varying numbers of students, so that their scores cover a wide enough range. Standardization refers to technical qualities of the tests, not a standard and precisely defined body of knowledge that they measure.

## standards

***What it means:*** Expectations for teaching and learning.

***Example:*** A broad standard: Students should have a good working understanding of the three branches of the United States government. A narrower standard: Students should know how many members of Congress there are and be able to name the agencies represented in the president's Cabinet.

### What you need to know about it

We all agree, don't we, that we want to have high expectations of our students and do everything we can to ensure that they learn? Why, then, are there such big battles over standards? Perhaps it's because the term has multiple meanings, so that we're talking past each other.

To politicians, standards mean that the taxpayers will get their money's worth: teachers and students will work hard, and we'll check up on them to make sure. As a result, our country will prosper economically. To educational traditionalists, standards mean that the curriculum will be rigorous and back-to-basics, with the result measured by traditional kinds of tests. To professional organizations like the National Council of Teachers of English and National Council of Teachers of Mathematics, standards mean working hard to establish consensus among classroom teachers and other experts in the field as to what constitutes best practice. And to classroom teachers, standards mean ensuring that every student has the opportunity to learn, and does learn, with much common ground but reflecting an understanding that students differ in their interests, capacities, and starting points.

These meanings shouldn't necessarily be inconsistent, but in fact they lead to very different policy stances. An example is the decision of the U.S. Department of Education in 1994 to not renew funding for the International Reading Association and National Council of Teachers of English to develop standards for the English language arts, since they felt the work in progress focused too much on process and learning activities and not enough on specifics like defining what students should know and be able to do (Diegmueller 1994; see **Professional Organizations**).

Let's try to clarify, then, what we might mean when we refer to standards. (Also, see Falk 2000, for an excellent discussion of standards in general and sensible approaches to standards as a learning tool in particular.)

*Opportunity-to-learn* standards recognize that students need appropriate chances to achieve our expectations. Following this principle, the International Reading Association has recently issued a document that calls for a commitment to principles such as "well-prepared teachers who keep their skills up to date through effective professional development" and "reading instruction that makes meaningful use of [student's] first language skills" (IRA 2000). In a sense, these standards, which usually imply that adequate funding is necessary to achieve them, must underlie all other standards.

*Content standards* refer to what the curriculum should look like. These can be broad, such as NCTM's standard (1989) that students should "develop number sense for whole numbers, fractions, decimals, integers, and rational numbers" (87) but often become very specific, such as Virginia's standard that third-graders should "create and solve problems that involve multiplication of two whole numbers, one factor 99 or less and the second factor 5 or less" and eighth-graders, "given a whole number from 0 to 100, will identify it as a perfect square or find the two consecutive whole numbers between which the square root lies" (Virginia Board of Education 1995). Typically, the standards developed by professional organizations don't mandate specific content as often or with as much detail as those developed by state departments of education. Some extreme examples of the latter end up sounding more like blueprints for test construction rather than thoughtful plans for what curriculum should be like.

*Outcome or performance standards* focus on what students should know or be able to do; they're the most popular politically, and carry the greatest potential for abuse. Thoughtful outcome standards would provide intelligent assessment, improve accountability, and provide direction for future instruction. However, if they don't take individual differences into account, if they overfocus on narrow measures like standardized tests, or if they carry inappropriately high stakes, they risk distorting the entire educational process.

Some kinds of outcomes depend more on individual differences than others. For instance, take a high school Algebra II class. Presumably all students entering the class would have passed Algebra I, so you could assume a relatively common starting point, although there will always of course be differences in the depth of their understanding and in their mathematical interest and abilities. But one could hope that if teaching was successful and the students were relatively involved in their learning, everyone would finish Algebra II with similar understandings.

But what about third-grade reading? Every elementary teacher knows that students enter a grade with widely different reading abilities. In third grade, it typically ranges from nonreaders to those able to read any book that interests them. Also, outcomes for reading are much harder to define than for algebra, since the learning is a development in ability and strategies rather than an acquisition of knowledge.

A standard, therefore, that every student finish third grade reading at "third-grade level," however that's defined (see **Grade Level**), is going to be unrealistic for some students and not challenging enough for others. We need to be very cautious indeed in defining outcome standards and how they're applied.

## test security

**What it means:** Ensuring that test results aren't compromised by overt cheating.

**Example:** Keeping test booklets locked up until test day.

**What you need to know about it**

From your own experiences as a student, you know that test questions are usually kept secret. Teachers who use multiple-choice tests either make sure that students don't keep a copy of the test or rewrite the test every year. There are periodic scandals when security for high-stakes standardized tests like the SAT is breached. The reasons are obvious: If some test-takers have had advance access to test questions, the possibility of cheating means that the scores can't be relied on.

Test security for major gatekeeper tests like the SAT and those for admission to law and medical schools is particularly tight. These tests, which are usually paid for by the test-takers, who are there voluntarily, are kept in a secured location. Students must show photo IDs and are seated apart from each other and proctored. Multiple versions are used to prevent copying from a neighbor, and all test materials are collected to ensure that no leaks take place. This protects not only the colleges and programs that will use the test scores to make decisions, but honest test-takers who need to know that the system is fair and has integrity.

Procedures for in-school standardized tests, which are paid for by the school and required of students, should have similar safeguards but in practice may not. When violations occur, they're most often committed not by the test-takers but by teachers and administrators who may, without even realizing what's wrong with it, use preknowledge of the test to teach to it, even if not providing students with outright coaching. Although this may be done out of an innocent desire to have students do well and increase their test scores, is it really any different in outcome from a student who's broken into a teacher's desk to peek at the math final?

We think of test security as being violated primarily by those who are taking the test and would therefore benefit from seeing it beforehand, but when teachers are being judged by their students' test scores, they also have an interest in higher scores. Schools shouldn't be casual about following the established standards of security for a particular test, and state tests need to come with guidelines for ensuring that test scores aren't contaminated by teachers who use advance knowledge of a test to shape their curriculum.

Perhaps part of the problem is with the concept of secure tests in the first place. Wiggins (1993) makes a persuasive case that in order to be fair, assessment should be as transparent as possible to its subjects. When a test is held under tight security, there's no opportunity to see what questions you missed or even ensure that the scoring was legitimate and accurate. (For this latter reason, many states and ETS now publish test items after they've been used.) What Wiggins envisions would, however, require a move away from tests that measure factual information to assessment that measures knowledge and abilities more holistically. As long as traditional testing systems are in place, they need to be kept secure in order to be fair.

## test specifications

***What it means:*** Technical requirements for test developers.

***Example:*** 70 percent of test items should be four-answer multiple choice and 30 percent true/false.

### What you need to know about it

When a state institutes a testing program, it's common to contract with an outside firm to create the test. Looking at a set of specifications for such a test provides a revealing look at how they're conceptualized and developed. The state of Virginia (Virginia Department of Education 1997; all material referred to here comes from their website) has made the guidelines for their tests available on the Internet. (Although copyright considerations prevent me from quoting directly, material can be seen at the website.)

I looked at two specific tests that reflect different kinds of curriculum: Third-grade English (with reading and writing subtests) involves developing abilities and strategies, while fifth-grade history and social science focuses (at least in Virginia) more on factual content. I also looked at sample test items that have been released for these two subject areas to see how the specifications played out in practice.

First of all, the format of the tests is multiple-choice, which drastically limits the scope and quality of the assessment. The reading test items are all questions following a reading passage, while the writing test items use a writing sample to create test items related to planning, composition, revising, and editing. Many of them ask students to choose the answer that will best correct an error in a mock piece of student writing. The history and social science test sample items almost all involve factual recall.

The test specifications are geared very closely to the state standards, and reflect a very technical orientation, in the sense that the standards break knowledge and strategies down into small pieces (such as the use of beginning and ending consonants in reading, the use of declarative and interrogatory sentences in writing, and knowledge of specific Civil War events in history), to which the test developers (in this case, Harcourt Brace Educational Measurement) are then asked to target test items. In the reading test, 40 percent of the twenty-five test items address word analysis, 40 percent understanding of text, and 20 percent elements of literature. The writing test items are 65 percent planning, composing, and revision, and 35 percent editing. The forty items on the history and social science test cover mostly history and geography, but 25 percent deal with civics and economics.

Virginia's standards have been notorious for their length, complexity, and age-inappropriateness. For instance, the fourth-grade history standard to which the fifth-grade test is written reads, in part, "The student will evaluate the social, political, and economic life in Virginia from the Reconstruction Period to the 20th century, with emphasis on a) the Reconstruction Period and its impact on politics and government, the economy, demographics, and public opinion." One envisions sophisticated classes almost at the level of a graduate seminar! However, when one goes from the standard to the curriculum guides, where the information is presented as a series of facts, it becomes apparent that students won't be asked to think about the topic, but merely be exposed to information about it. Then a look at the sample test items which, for fifth-grade history and social science, are all factual recall except for one simple map interpretation item, leads to the conclusion that low-level memorizing is the real message of this apparently advanced curriculum.

Looking at the sample test items for third-grade English is equally discouraging. Students' ability to describe characters in fiction is reduced to applying the appropriate choice of four adjectives; the ability to focus on a single topic while writing is reduced to selecting the off-topic sentence for an artificial student composition. These tasks seem far removed from the goal.

In an attempt to develop criterion-referenced tests, Virginia and other states have taken a different path than that of norm-referenced tests, where items are developed and chosen in part according to how well they serve to rank test-takers. (See **Criterion- and Norm-Referenced Tests**.) However, creating tests through a process of breaking knowledge down into small pieces—that are then further fragmented by turning them into multiple-choice items—waters down the ideal of high standards into a virtual parody of itself.

## testing teachers

*What it means:*  Requiring some formal measure, beyond successful completion of a teacher education program, to obtain a teaching license.

*Example:*  The PRAXIS exams from the Educational Testing Service, the C-BEST, and various state-designed tests.

### What you need to know about it

In most states, prospective teachers are required to take tests that measure content knowledge, as well as passing tests of reading, writing, and mathematics. These tests are often required before entering a teacher education program. However, ETS has eliminated the Pre-Professional Skills Test (PPST), which was intended to assess students at the conclusion of teacher education programs. Current thinking about evaluating beginning teachers has shifted from testing to broader criteria.

A number of professional bodies are devoted to establishing standards for teacher quality and for teacher education programs. The Interstate New Teacher Assessment and Support Consortium (INTASC) (1992; see http://www.ccsso.org/intasc.html) has developed a series of standards for prospective teachers, which are consistent with the standards for colleges of education used for accreditation by the National Council for Accreditation of Teacher Education (NCATE). For master teachers at mid-career, national certification through the National Board for Professional Teaching Standards continues the process. These standards are thoughtful, focused on both knowledge and outcomes, and reflect a broad consensus within the profession that teacher quality is too important to measure with a test and must be looked at multidimensionally.

Unfortunately, some states haven't gotten this message, or choose to adopt a simplistic but flashy approach, as Massachusetts has done with its widely criticized teacher exam. The reading and writing tests, which included the candidates taking dictation from a difficult-to-hear tape of *The Federalist Papers*, were reviewed by testing experts, who found them lacking in the most basic principles of test reliability and validity and recommended that their use be immediately suspended (Haney, et al. 1999). Not only did the tests have huge margins of error, but their content was highly questionable and both testing conditions and scoring were problematic. The tests were developed by a company with a poor performance record in test development.

Even less useful is the idea of using standardized tests to evaluate practicing teachers, as was introduced by both a Democratic governor (Bill Clinton) and a Republican one (George W. Bush). A poor substitute for constructive ways to identify and take action with ineffective teachers, such approaches may be politically popular but are merely expensive hollow gestures.

## validity[5]

**What it means:** Does a test measure what it says it does?

**Example:** Do those who pass the driver's test know the rules of the road when they drive?

5. Hopkins (1998), was a useful source of information on this topic.

### What you need to know about it

Validity is one of the two important cornerstones in establishing the quality of a test or similar measure. (For the other, see **Reliability**.) For the purposes of educational testing, a few different kinds of validity are relevant. (Also, it's important to be aware that a test can't be valid unless it's reliable; that is, it is likely to result in consistent scores when taken more than once.)

### Content validity

If we want a test that measures knowledge of American history, it should obviously be made up of questions related to the topic. Content validity usually refers to a systematic attempt to ensure that the range of content is appropriately covered, and that background knowledge or abilities irrelevant to the content (such as very strong reading proficiency) aren't required, and so on. When states write test specifications that designate how many questions should be included per topic on a subject area, they're following standards of content validity. (See **Test Specifications**.) Standardized test developers usually try to achieve content validity that's suitable for a wide range of educational settings, so would therefore avoid questions about a single state's history on a national test.

One problem in establishing content validity in educational settings is that not all important content areas can be measured by all test instruments, particularly multiple-choice tests. So, for instance, Virginia's specifications for English tests don't cover the standards related to oral language and technology (Virginia Department of Education 1997). In a sense, such limitations on a test's content validity shouldn't be a problem, as long as it's acknowledged, but if the schools' and public's focus is on raising test scores rather than on achieving *all* the goals of the curriculum, important areas of learning will be neglected.

Also, too much validity may be assumed in some cases. For instance, good readers have been known to do poorly on phonics tests.

Reading may be defined operationally in part as the ability to do well on a phonics test, but this doesn't necessarily apply to everyone.

### Concurrent validity

Concurrent validity is a reasonable way of determining the validity of a test through a comparison with another test. For instance, the developer of a new reading comprehension test who can show that it produces scores very similar to that of a well-established reading test can then fairly claim validity for the new test and perhaps market it as achieving the same results at a lower cost or in less time. Concurrent validity can also be established between a test and other kinds of measures, such as teacher assessment of a student, or a multiple-choice spelling test may correlate strongly to a dictated list of spelling words.

One danger, however, is in losing sight of what's really being measured. For instance, a reading comprehension test may do very well at predicting how well a student would do on another reading comprehension test, but may or may not connect with how well that student can discuss what she's read with a teacher, formulate her own responses to it, and so on. If we aren't careful about the need to think directly about true content validity, reading comprehension can end up being defined merely as the ability to do well on reading comprehension tests.

### Predictive validity

Predictive validity comes into play when a test is used to predict the likelihood of some future performance. How well is this student likely to do in college (the SAT exam)? Does this person know his subject matter well enough to teach it (the PRAXIS exams from the Educational Testing Service)? For such tests to be used fairly, they need to have a reasonable level of predictive validity and to be used flexibly. For instance, strict SAT cutoff scores are rarely appropriate for college admissions. The lower the level of predictive validity for a gatekeeper test (a typical correlation is 0.35; National Commission on Testing and Public Policy 1990), the more likely it is to produce not only false positives (people admitted to a program or profession who are unlikely to do well) but a large number of false negatives as well (people who would have been successful but who are kept out). Questions of validity are crucial to accurate and fair test use; teachers and others who play a part in their use should not only be aware of this but be vigilant on behalf of their students.

## what should an educated person know?

**What it means:** Expectations for what knowledge citizens should have.

**Example:** Can you say a little bit about desegregation, the periodic table, and Hawthorne?

### What you need to know about it

In a sense, the whole discussion about educational standards is an attempt to define what an educated person should know. I'd like, however, to consider one aspect of this question: knowledge as content versus knowledge as process. This has been a subject of discussion and contention for a long time, and was given a particular focus by the publication of E. D. Hirsch's *Cultural Literacy* in 1987. Hirsch, best-known for his list of 5,000 or so names, dates, terms, and concepts that an educated person should know, is a highly visible advocate for the importance of a strong common knowledge base. Indeed, he feels it's essential for a lively, socially fluid democracy. Often seen in opposition to this view is a process approach to learning and standards, where what's important is not so much the content of what's learned, but habits of thought, how to carry out research, developing interests, and a passion for learning, and so on.

These two views of learning aren't really, of course, diametrically antithetical, and most educators agree that both are important, but standards and curriculum models often emphasize one or the other. Hirsch's content model is often associated with a conservative, back-to-basics stance and with standards developed by state departments of education. (Hirsch's influence is seen especially strongly in his home state of Virginia.) A more process-oriented model is often seen in standards developed by professional organizations in fields such as English language arts, mathematics, and history. (See **Professional Organizations**.) The content people often view the process people as fuzzy-minded, while the process people see the content people as narrow and old-fashioned.

I'd like to propose a truce; a possible combining of the best of both models. Hirsch's list (random entries: amino acids, e pluribus unum, protective tariff, stanza) has been criticized as a horrible, Trivial Pursuit version of what education should all be about, as well as reflecting a Euro-American cultural bias. The list could certainly stand some tinkering (see Simonson and Walker 1988, for a culturally diverse addendum), but I think it is quite reasonable to hope that citizens should have some common ground in our knowledge of fields like science, history, geography, and the arts. When I look at Hirsch's list, I have at least a nodding familiarity with most of what's on it (and a nodding familiarity is all he thinks is necessary), and I'm glad that I do.

The big problem, however, is Hirsch's idea of how you get there. His publications have become a mini-industry, with a series of volumes on *What Your 1st [2nd, 3rd, etc.] Grader Needs to Know* as well as dictionaries of cultural literacy, software, and so on. Unfortunately, these books are dull compendiums that distort and isolate the original information and works that they are intended to "cover." For instance, the third-grade book (Hirsch 1992) summarizes *Alice in Wonderland* in three pages, with only four of the original Tenniel illustrations. The point, obviously, shouldn't be to gain a nodding acquaintance with this children's classic through reading a summary of it, but through reading the original in all the glory of its story, language, and art. History, geography, science, mathematics, and the arts are similarly trivialized and condensed in Hirsch's mini-encyclopedia for third grade.

But when I think about how I learned what I know from Hirsch's list, it sure wasn't like this! It was through voracious reading (supported by good libraries, developing interests that I had resources available to pursue, talking to people, and so on). I believe that this would be true for most people who are familiar with much of what's on Hirsch's list. So here's how we combine the best of both models: We work to develop students who are voracious readers, discussers, and thinkers, give them lots to read and talk about, fill up the school and public libraries and keep them open long hours with generous borrowing privileges, and involve parents in all of it. Students will end up not only with the mental habits and abilities of educated people but with a ton of knowledge as well.

## where do we go from here?

Some say tests will continue to become a bigger and more pervasive part of our educational system. At the time of my writing this, President George W. Bush's educational legislation requiring state testing of students in grades three through eight had recently been approved by Congress, lending credence to this view. Others feel that as parents and taxpayers see what extensive testing really looks like, particularly if large numbers of middle-class children don't pass, they'll rise up in protest and the entire apparatus will self-destruct. Reading the news lends support to either or both views. Well, predicting the future is always foolhardy, so I won't even try. Instead, I'll offer some ideas about how you can use the information contained in this book.

### *Help your students become test-wise.*

I mean this on two levels. First, particularly if they're faced with high-stakes tests, they should have the legitimate and ethical advantage of knowing everything from how to fill in an answer sheet accurately (particularly for younger students) and how to pace yourself effectively. And I think students would also be well-served by understanding some of the concepts and issues underlying testing and some of the problems in their use. For instance, even elementary-school students would benefit from an exploration of how answering comprehension questions is different from discussing what you've read. Older students could learn about reliability and validity and even research the extent to which their state's tests achieve them. How about a high-school civics class' exploration of the politics of testing, or of ethical standards for testing and how well their state preserves them?

### *Help parents become test-wise.*

I opened this book by mentioning that a group of parents I spoke to about testing and standards was surprised at much of what they learned, which they had never heard from the school or from the state department of education, although a good deal of other information had been provided to them. What was so surprising to them? A number of notions: that grade-level equivalent scores don't mean what you think they do; that passing scores are often set arbitrarily; that groups and individuals should be assessed differently.

What currently annoys you most about the tests your students are required to take? Are parents aware of the issue? If not, consider helping them share your knowledge through a presentation, a brief article in your parent newsletter, or individual conversations.

### *Work to protect students who score poorly on standardized tests.*

Students who are struggling in school are often humiliated by the poor scores they receive on standardized tests. The scores, of course, don't even provide any new information about these students; they just make them feel bad and worry their parents. Students need to know that what matters is their own learning, not how they compare to others or to an external standard on a test. We therefore need to avoid emphasizing tests when we talk to students; instead, treat them as a necessary evil that has little to do with the real life of the classroom. (This approach will also benefit students who test well, who sometimes don't value growing as learners when they know they can get high test scores with little effort.)

### *Work to make sure your school system uses appropriate testing practices.*

Use available resources (Heubert and Hauser 1999; Michigan Merit Award 2000; and the Appendix of this book) to examine whether your state, district, and school follow generally accepted standards for test development and administration. If not, let someone know. Write a letter to the editor or an op-ed piece, or work with your teacher support group or union to push for change.

Unfortunately, whistle-blowing can be dangerous; when Portland, Oregon, teacher Bill Bigelow (1999a) wrote an op-ed piece criticizing some items on a pilot state social studies test, the state superintendent of instruction allegedly asked his school district to fire him (Bigelow, 1999b). Chicago teacher George Schmidt bravely published an entire Chicago test in his newspaper *Substance* (Schmidt 1999) and not only lost his job but is enduring a $1 million lawsuit. (*Substance* can be ordered from 5132 W. Bertram Avenue, Chicago, IL 60641.) But both of these cases involved violation of test security; procedural and ethical challenges are just as valid and less likely to elicit reprisals.

### Connect with others locally and nationally.

FairTest's website, as mentioned earlier, can lead you to those in your state who are working on testing issues, and its Assessment Reform Network listserv can bring you daily emails from activists and others interested in testing issues. (See **Internet resources**.) Teachers, students, and parents all over the country are taking action in a variety of ways; you don't have to act alone.

### Resist all temptation to teach to the test.

No more cramming in as much curriculum as you can by April since the tests are given in early May; devoting several weeks to drill and review; not letting a student teacher go solo in the month before test time; covering a topic only because it's on the test; covering a topic less creatively than you normally would because it's on the test; letting the test outweigh other sources of your thinking about curriculum. Instead, develop your curriculum around what you think your students should know and how they should learn it, with the satisfaction that not only are you providing them with the best education you're capable of, you're avoiding a slippery slope of unethical testing practices.

### Send me a note.

You can reach me at wildes@pdx.edu, or through Heinemann. Let me know if you have questions about what you've read about in this book, and how you've been able to use the information to support kids. After all, supporting kids—helping and nurturing them in all ways possible—is always our first consideration.

# References

BERLINER, DAVID C., and BRUCE J. BIDDLE. 1995. *The Manufactured Crisis: Myths, Fraud, and the Attack on America's Public Schools.* Reading, MA: Addison-Wesley.

BIGELOW, BILL. 1999a. "Social Studies Tests from Hell." *Rethinking Schools* 13 (3). Accessed online at <http://www.rethinkingschools.org>. Also reprinted as "Tests from Hell" in *Failing Our Kids: Why the Testing Craze Won't Fix Our Schools,* edited by Kathy Swope and Barbara Miner, pp. 46–47. Milwaukee, WI: Rethinking Schools.

———. 1999b. "Testing Against Democracy." *Rethinking Schools* 13 (3). Accessed online at <http://www.rethinkingschools.org/Archives/13_03/hellsid.htm>.

BRACEY, GERALD W. 1997. *Setting the Record Straight: Responses to Misconceptions About Public Education in the United States.* Alexandria, VA: Association for Supervision and Curriculum Development.

———. 2000a. *Bail Me Out! Handling Difficult Data and Tough Questions About Public Schools.* Thousand Oaks, CA: Corwin.

———. 2000b. *Thinking About Tests and Testing: A Short Primer in "Assessment Literacy."* Washington, DC: American Youth Policy Forum. Accessed online at <http://www.aypf.org/pubs.htm>; follow the link to OnLine Publications.

BURNS, PAUL C. 1998. *Informal Reading Inventory: Preprimer to Twelfth Grade.* 5th ed. Boston: Houghton Mifflin.

CALKINS, LUCY M., KATE MONTGOMERY, and DONNA SANTMAN, with BEVERLY FALK. 1998. *A Teacher's Guide to Standardized Reading Tests: Knowledge Is Power.* Portsmouth, NH: Heinemann.

CAMPBELL, JAY R., CLYDE M. REESE, CHRISTINE O'SULLIVAN, and JOHN A. DOSSEY. 1996. *NAEP 1994 Trends of Academic Progress.* Washington, DC: National Center for Education Statistics. ERIC Document Reproduction Service Document ED 402 356.

CANNELL, JOHN J. 1988. "Nationally Normed Elementary Achievement Testing in America's Public Schools: How All 50 States Are Above the National Average." *Educational Measurement: Issues and Practice* 7 (2):5–9.

———. 1989. *The "Lake Wobegon" Report: How Public Educators Cheat on Standardized Achievement Tests.* Daniels, WV: Friends for Education.

COHEN, MIRIAM. 1980. *First Grade Takes a Test.* New York: Greenwillow.

DIEGMUELLER, KAREN. 1994. "English Group Loses Funding for Standards." *Education Week* (30 March): Retrieved online at <http://www.edweek.org>.

DONAHUE, PATRICIA L., KRISTIN E. VOELKL, JAY R CAMPBELL, and JOHN MAZZEO. 1999. *NAEP 1998 Writing Report Card for the Nation and the States.* Washington, DC: National Center for Education Statistics.

FALK, BEVERLY. 2000. *The Heart of the Matter: Using Standards and Assessment to Learn.* Portsmouth, NH: Heinemann.

FINCHLER, JUDY. 2000. *Testing Miss Malarkey.* New York: Walker.

FRASER, STEVEN, ed. 1995. *The Bell Curve Wars: Race, Intelligence, and the Future of America.* New York: Basic Books.

GOODMAN, KENNETH S. 1998. "Who's Afraid of Whole Language? Politics, Paradigms, Pedagogy, and the Press." In *In Defense of Good Teaching: What Teachers Need to Know About the "Reading*

Wars," edited by Kenneth S. Goodman, pp. 3–37. York, ME: Stenhouse.

HALADYNA, THOMAS M., SUSAN B. NOLEN, and NANCY S. HAAS. 1991. "Raising Standardized Achievement Test Scores and the Origins of Test Score Pollution." *Educational Researcher* 20:2–7.

HANEY, WALT, CLARKE FOWLER, ANNE WHEELOCK, DAMIAN BEBELL, and NICOLE MALEC. 1999. "Less Truth Than Error? An Independent Study of the Massachusetts Teacher Tests." *Education Policy Analysis Archives* 7. Retrieved online at <http://olam.ed.asu.edu/epaa/v7n4>.

HANEY, WALTER M., GEORGE F. MADAUS, and ROBERT LYONS. 1993. *The Fractured Marketplace for Standardized Testing*. Boston: Kluwer.

HARMON, SUSAN. 2002. Personal communication.

HARRIS, JOSEPH. 2000. *Get Ready! For Standardized Tests (Grade 4)*. New York: McGraw-Hill. (With companion books, by various authors, for Grades 1 through 6.)

HARTOCOLLIS, ANEMONA. 1999. "Crossed Fingers: Liar, Liar, Pants on Fire." *New York Times,* 12 December. Retrieved online at <http://www.nytimes.com>.

———. 2000. "9 Educators Accused of Encouraging Students to Cheat." *New York Times*, 3 May. Retrieved online at <http://www.nytimes.com>.

HEGARTY, STEPHEN. 2000. "Officials Dodge the FCAT Challenge." *St. Petersburg (FL) Times*, 13 February. Retrieved online at <http://pgasb.pgarchiver.com/sptimes>.

HERMANS, KEN. 2001. Email communication.

HERRNSTEIN, RICHARD J., and CHARLES MURRAY. 1994. *The Bell Curve: Intelligence and Class Structure in American Life*. New York: Free Press.

HEUBERT, JAY P., and ROBERT M. HAUSER. 1999. *High Stakes: Testing for Tracking, Promotion, and Graduation*. Washington, DC: National Academy Press.

Hill, Clifford, and Eric Larson. 2002. *Children and Reading Tests (Advances in Discourse Processes, Vol. LXV)*. Stamford, CT: Ablex.

Hirsch, E. D., Jr. 1987. *Cultural Literacy: What Every American Needs to Know*. New York: Houghton Mifflin.

———, ed. 1992. *What Your 3rd Grader Needs to Know: Fundamentals of a Good Third-Grade Education*. New York: Doubleday. (Similar books are available for other grade levels.)

Hopkins, Kenneth D. 1998. *Educational and Psychological Measurement and Evaluation*. 8th ed. Boston: Allyn and Bacon.

International Reading Association. 2000. *Making a Difference Means Making It Different: Honoring Children's Rights of Excellent Reading Instruction* (Policy statement). Retrieved online at <http://www.reading.org/policy/MADMMID.html>.

Interstate New Teacher Assessment and Support Consortium. 1992. *Model Standards for Beginning Teacher Licensing and Development: A Resource for State Dialogue*. Retrieved online at <http://www.ccsso.org/intascst.html>.

Jencks, Christopher, and Meredith Phillips, eds. 1998. *The Black-White Test Score Gap*. Washington, DC: The Brookings Institution.

Kincheloe, Joe L., Shirley R. Steinberg, and Aaron D. Gresson III. 1996. *Measured Lies: The Bell Curve Examined*. New York: St. Martin's.

Kohn, Alfie. 1993. *Punished by Rewards: The Problem with Gold Stars, Incentive Plans, A's, Praise, and Other Bribes*. Boston: Houghton Mifflin.

———. 1999. *The Schools Our Children Deserve: Moving Beyond Traditional Classrooms and "Tougher Standards."* Boston: Houghton Mifflin.

————. 2000. *The Case Against Standardized Testing: Raising the Scores, Ruining the Schools.* Portsmouth, NH: Heinemann.

LAVERGNE, GARY M. 2001. "Is This the End for the SAT?" *New York Times,* 4 March. Retrieved online at <www.nytimes.com>.

LEMANN, NICHOLAS. 1999. *The Big Test: The Secret History of the American Meritocracy.* New York: Farrar, Straus & Giroux.

MCNEIL, LINDA M. 2000. *Contradictions of School Reform: Educational Costs of Standardized Testing.* New York: Routledge.

MCNEIL, LINDA, and ANGELA VALENZUELA. 2000. "The Harmful Impact of the TAAS System of Testing in Texas: Beneath the Accountability Rhetoric." Cambridge, MA: The Civil Rights Project, Harvard University. Accessed online at <http://www.law.harvard.edu>; follow the link to publications.

MEIER, DEBORAH. 1981, Fall. "Why Reading Tests Don't Test Reading." *Dissent* 28: 457–66.

MICHIGAN MERIT AWARD BOARD. 2000. Test Administration Ethics Procedures (Resolution 2000-14). Accessed online at <http://www.MeritAward.state.mi.us/merit/meap/ethics.htm>.

NASH, GARY B., CHARLOTTE CRABTREE, and ROSS E. DUNN. 1997. *History on Trial: Culture Wars and the Teaching of the Past.* New York: Knopf.

NATIONAL COMMISSION ON EXCELLENCE IN EDUCATION. 1983. *A Nation at Risk: The Imperative for Educational Reform.* Washington, DC: National Commission on Excellence in Education. ERIC Document Reproduction Service Document ED 226 006y.

NATIONAL COMMISSION ON TESTING AND PUBLIC POLICY. 1990. *From Gatekeeper to Gateway: Transforming Testing in America.* Chestnut Hill, MA: Boston College (National Commission on Testing and Public Policy).

NATIONAL COUNCIL OF TEACHERS OF MATHEMATICS. 1989. *Curriculum and Evaluation Standards for School Mathematics.* Reston, VA: NCTM.

OHANIAN, SUSAN. 1998. *Standards, Plain English, and the Ugly Duckling: Lessons About What Teachers Really Do*. Bloomington, IN: Phi Delta Kappan Educational Foundation.

———. 1999. *One Size Fits Few: The Folly of Educational Standards*. Portsmouth, NH: Heinemann.

———. 2000. "You Say Stakeholder; I Say Robber Baron." *Language Arts* 78:148–57.

OREGON DEPARTMENT OF EDUCATION. 1999. *State of Oregon: Teaching and Learning to Standards, 1999–2000*. Salem, Oregon Department of Education.

OWINGS, WILLIAM A., and SUSAN MAGLIARO. 1998. "Grade Retention: A History of Failure." *Educational Leadership* 56:86–8.

PARIS, SCOTT G., THERESA A. LAWTON, JULIANNE C. TURNER, and JODIE L. ROTH. 1991. "A Developmental Perspective on Standardized Achievement Testing." *Educational Researcher* 20:12–20, 40.

RAVITCH, DIANE. 1996. "Defining Literacy Downward." *New York Times*, 28 August. Retrieved online at <http://www.nytimes.com>.

RAVITCH, DIANE, and CHESTER E. FINN, JR. 1988. *What Do Our 17-Year-Olds Know? A Report on the First National Assessment of History and Literature*. New York: Harper & Row.

ROTHSTEIN, RICHARD. 1998. *The Way We Were? The Myths and Realities of America's Student Achievement*. New York: The Century Foundation.

———. 2000. "Lessons: Positive Trends Hidden in SAT and ACT Scores." *New York Times*, 29 August, B8.

———. 2001a. "Lessons: Test Here and There, Not Everywhere." *New York Times*, 6 June, B8.

———. 2001b. "Lessons: In Standardized Tests, Standards Vary." *New York Times*, 19 July, B9.

SACKS, PETER. 1999. *Standardized Minds: The High Price of America's Testing Culture and What We Can Do to Change It*. Cambridge, MA: Perseus.

SCHMIDT, GEORGE. 1999. "Chicago Moves to Teacher Proof its High School Curriculum with CASE Tests." *Substance 24* (5 & 6):17–32.

SCHRAG, PETER. 2000. "High Stakes Are for Tomatoes." *The Atlantic Monthly*, October. Retrieved online at <http://www.theatlantic.com>.

SEUSS, DR., and JACK PRELUTSKY. 1998. *Hooray for Diffendoofer Day!* New York: Knopf.

SHANAHAN, TIMOTHY. 2000. "Phonics Is Only One Ingredient" (Letters). *The Indianapolis Star,* 7 May. Retrieved online at <http://www.starnews.com>.

SHANNON, PATRICK. 1996. "Mad as Hell." *Language Arts* 73:14–19.

SHAVER, KATHERINE. 1997. "A Mixed Report Card on Student Testing." *The Washington Post*, 14 October. Retrieved online at <http://www.washingtonpost.com>.

SIMONSON, RICK, and SCOTT WALKER, eds. 1988. *The Graywolf Annual Five Multi-Cultural Literacy.* Saint Paul, MN: Graywolf.

SMITH, FRANK. 1998. *The Book of Learning and Forgetting.* New York: Teachers College Press.

SMITH, MARY LEE. 1991. "Put to the Test: The Effects of External Testing on Teachers." *Educational Researcher* 20:8–11.

SWOPE, KATHY, and BARBARA MINER, eds. 2000. *Failing Our Kids: Why the Testing Craze Won't Fix Our Schools.* Milwaukee, WI: Rethinking Schools.

TALK OF THE NATION (radio program). 2000. "Cheating Schools." January 6. Washington, DC: National Public Radio.

TAYLOR, KATHE, and SHERRY WALTON. 1998. *Children at the Center: A Workshop Approach to Standardized Test Preparation, K–8.* Portsmouth, NH: Heinemann.

THOMAS, EVAN, and PAT WINGERT. 2000. "Bitter Lessons." *Newsweek* 135 (19 June):50ff.

"TRUTH ABOUT READING" (editorial). 2000. *The Indianapolis Star,* 2 May. Retrieved online at <http://www.starnews.com>.

VIRGINIA (COMMONWEALTH OF) BOARD OF EDUCATION. 1995. *Mathematics Standards of Learning for Virginia Public Schools.* Retrieved online at <http://www.pen.k12.va.us/go.Sols/math.html>.

VIRGINIA (COMMONWEALTH OF) DEPARTMENT OF EDUCATION. 1997. *Standards of Learning Assessment Program: Test Blueprints.* Retrieved online at <http://www.pen.k12.va.us/VDOE/Assessment/soltests>.

WIGGINS, GRANT. 1993. *Assessing Student Performance: Exploring the Purpose and Limits of Testing.* San Francisco: Jossey-Bass.

WILDE, SANDRA. 2000. *Miscue Analysis Made Easy: Building on Student Strengths.* Portsmouth, NH: Heinemann.

WILGORIN, JODI, and JACQUES STEINBERG. 2000. "Under Pressure: A Special Report (Even for Sixth Graders, College Looms)." *New York Times,* 3 July. Retrieved online at <www.nytimes.com>.

WISE, ARTHUR. 1979. *Legislated Learning.* Berkeley, CA: University of California.

# Appendix

AERA Position Statement
Concerning
High-Stakes Testing
in PreK-12 Education

The American Educational Research Association (AERA) is the nation's largest professional organization devoted to the scientific study of education. The AERA seeks to promote educational policies and practices that credible scientific research has shown to be beneficial, and to discourage those found to have negative effects. From time to time, the AERA issues statements setting forth its research-based position on educational issues of public concern. One such current issue is the increasing use of high-stakes tests as instruments of educational policy.

This position statement on high-stakes testing is based on the 1999 Standards for Educational and Psychological Testing. The Standards represent a professional consensus concerning sound and appropriate test use in education and psychology. They are sponsored and endorsed by the AERA together with the American Psychological Association (APA) and the National Council on Measurement in Education (NCME). This statement is intended as a guide and a caution to policy makers, testing professionals, and test users involved in high-stakes testing programs. However, the Standards remain the most comprehensive and authoritative statement by the AERA concerning appropriate test use and interpretation.

Many states and school districts mandate testing programs to gather data about student achievement over time and to hold schools and students accountable. Certain uses of achievement test results are termed "high stakes" if they carry serious consequences for students or for educators. Schools may be judged according to the school-wide average scores of their students. High school-wide scores may bring public praise or financial rewards; low scores may bring public embarrassment or heavy sanctions. For individual students, high scores may bring a special diploma attesting to exceptional academic accomplishment; low scores may result in students being held back in grade or denied a high school diploma.

These various high-stakes testing applications are enacted by policy makers with the intention of improving education. For example, it is hoped that setting high standards of achievement will inspire greater effort on the part of students, teachers, and educational administrators. Reporting of test results may also be beneficial in directing public attention to gross achievement disparities among schools or among student groups. However, if high-stakes testing programs are implemented in circumstances where educational resources are inadequate or where tests lack sufficient reliability and validity for their intended purposes, there is potential for serious harm. Policy makers and the public may be misled by spurious test score increases unrelated to any fundamental educational improvement; students may be placed at increased risk of educational failure and dropping out; teachers may be blamed or punished for inequitable resources over which they have no control; and curriculum and instruction may be severely distorted if high test scores per se, rather than learning, become the overriding goal of classroom instruction.

This statement sets forth a set of conditions essential to sound implementation of high-stakes educational testing programs. It is the position of the AERA that every high-stakes achievement testing program in education should meet all of the following conditions:

## Protection Against High-Stakes Decisions Based on a Single Test

Decisions that affect individual students' life chances or educational opportunities should not be made on the basis of test scores alone. Other relevant information should be taken into account to enhance the overall validity of such decisions. As a minimum assurance of fairness, when tests are used as part of making high-stakes decisions for individual students such as promotion to the next grade or high school graduation, students must be afforded multiple opportunities to pass the test. More importantly, when there is credible evidence that a test score may not adequately reflect a student's true proficiency, alternative acceptable means should be provided by which to demonstrate attainment of the tested standards.

## Adequate Resources and Opportunity to Learn

When content standards and associated tests are introduced as a reform to change and thereby improve current practice, opportunities to access appropriate materials and retraining consistent with the intended changes should be provided before schools, teachers, or students are sanctioned for failing to meet the new standards. In particular, when testing is used for individual student accountability or certification, students must have had a meaningful opportunity to learn the tested content and cognitive processes. Thus, it must be shown that the tested content has been incorporated into the curriculum, materials, and instruction students are provided before high-stakes consequences are imposed for failing examination.

## Validation for Each Separate Intended Use

Tests valid for one use may be invalid for another. Each separate use of a high-stakes test, for individual certification, for school evaluation, for curricular improvement, for increasing student motivation, or for other uses requires a separate evaluation of the strengths and limitations of both the testing program and the test itself.

### Full Disclosure of Likely Negative Consequences of High-Stakes Testing Programs

Where credible scientific evidence suggests that a given type of testing program is likely to have negative side effects, test developers and users should make a serious effort to explain these possible effects to policy makers.

### Alignment Between the Test and the Curriculum

Both the content of the test and the cognitive processes engaged in taking the test should adequately represent the curriculum. High-stakes tests should not be limited to that portion of the relevant curriculum that is easiest to measure. When testing is for school accountability or to influence the curriculum, the test should be aligned with the curriculum as set forth in standards documents representing intended goals of instruction. Because high-stakes testing inevitably creates incentives for inappropriate methods of test preparation, multiple test forms should be used or new test forms should be introduced on a regular basis, to avoid a narrowing of the curriculum toward just the content sampled on a particular form.

### Validity of Passing Scores and Achievement Levels

When testing programs use specific scores to determine "passing" or to define reporting categories like "proficient," the validity of these specific scores must be established in addition to demonstrating the representativeness of the test content. To begin with, the purpose and meaning of passing scores or achievement levels must be clearly stated. There is often confusion, for example, among minimum competency levels (traditionally required for grade-to-grade promotion), grade level (traditionally defined as a range of scores around the national average on standardized tests), and "world-class" standards (set at the top of the distribution, anywhere from the 70th to the 99th percentile). Once the purpose is clearly established, sound and appropriate procedures must be followed in setting passing scores or proficiency levels. Finally, validity evidence must be gathered and reported, consistent with the stated purpose.

## Opportunities for Meaningful Remediation for Examinees Who Fail High-Stakes Tests

Examinees who fail a high-stakes test should be provided meaningful opportunities for remediation. Remediation should focus on the knowledge and skills the test is intended to address, not just the test performance itself. There should be sufficient time before retaking the test to assure that students have time to remedy any weaknesses discovered.

## Appropriate Attention to Language Differences Among Examinees

If a student lacks mastery of the language in which a test is given, then that test becomes, in part, a test of language proficiency. Unless a primary purpose of a test is to evaluate language proficiency, it should not be used with students who cannot understand the instructions or the language of the test itself. If English language learners are tested in English, their performance should be interpreted in the light of their language proficiency. Special accommodations for English language learners may be necessary to obtain valid scores.

## Appropriate Attention to Students with Disabilities

In testing individuals with disabilities, steps should be taken to ensure that the test score inferences accurately reflect the intended construct rather than any disabilities and their associated characteristics extraneous to the intent of the measurement.

## Careful Adherence to Explicit Rules for Determining Which Students Are to Be Tested

When schools, districts, or other administrative units are compared to one another or when changes in scores are tracked over time, there must be explicit policies specifying which students are to be tested and under what circumstances students may be exempted from testing. Such policies must be uniformly enforced to assure the validity of score comparisons. In addition, reporting of test score results should accurately portray the percentage of students exempted.

## Sufficient Reliability for Each Intended Use

Reliability refers to the accuracy or precision of test scores. It must be shown that scores reported for individuals or for schools are sufficiently accurate to support each intended interpretation. Accuracy should be examined for the scores actually used. For example, information about the reliability of raw scores may not adequately describe the accuracy of percentiles; information about the reliability of school means may be insufficient if scores for subgroups are also used in reaching decisions about schools.

## Ongoing Evaluation of Intended and Unintended Effects of High-Stakes Testing

With any high-stakes testing program, ongoing evaluation of both intended and unintended consequences is essential. In most cases, the governmental body that mandates the test should also provide resources for a continuing program of research and for dissemination of research findings concerning both the positive and the negative effects of the testing program.

## Adopted July 2000